A History of Moonville, Ohio
and a
Collection of its Haunting Tales

A History of Moonville, Ohio
and a
Collection of its Haunting Tales

William M. Cullen

COPYRIGHT © 2010 BY WILLIAM M. CULLEN.

ISBN: HARDCOVER   978-1-4500-3566-8
        SOFTCOVER   978-1-4500-3565-1

All rights reserved. No part of this book may be reproduced or transmitted in any form or by any means, electronic or mechanical, including photocopying, recording, or by any information storage and retrieval system, without permission in writing from the copyright owner.

This information, herein, is to be considered factual and accurate as it possibly can be. It is by no means the entire history since so much has been lost over time. However, this material is based on information gathered from the library archives, historical society archives and internet research. Therefore, the contents are meant to be as faithful to the original intent in which they were given and are given with the utmost reverence to its authenticity.

This book was printed in the United States of America.

To order additional copies of this book, contact:
Xlibris Corporation
1-888-795-4274
www.Xlibris.com
Orders@Xlibris.com
46801

CONTENTS

Introduction 7
A History of Moonville 11
A Collection of Moonville's Haunting Tales 28
    The Falling Brakemen 30
    A Miner 34
    Small Pox and the Brave Volunteer 35
    The Headless Conductor 38
    The Tall 'Dark' One 42
    The Haunting Ladies 45
    Murdered Men 48
    A Suicide 49
    A Bizarre Accident 49
    David's Story 50
    The Ohio Exploration Society 51
    A Boy Saved by a Ghost 52
Parting Thoughts 53
Directions to Moonville Tunnel 55
Bibliography 57
Index 61

Introduction

Once I read about Moonville in '*Weird Ohio*' I, too, became quite intrigued with its nearly forgotten history and its nearly forgotten ghost legends that surround this most tranquil but, yet, intriguing place in the backwoods of Ohio. It certainly has an eerie charm about it when you see this old abandon tunnel out in the remote woods.

You see dear reader I have always had a penchant for ghost stories since I was a kid back in my hometown of Portsmouth, Ohio. I grew up reading countless number of ghost stories, ranging from the more known—*Sleepy Hollow* by Washington Irving or *A Christmas Carol* by Charles Dickens, to the more obscure—*The Ghost with the Golden Casket* by Allan Cunningham or *The Phantom Train of Marshall Pass* by Charles Skinner.

But what I think what got me truly interested in ghosts, or ghost stories, was when I attended my local church—The United Methodist Church of Franklin Avenue—as a child and was taught by the good people there that when the body dies its internal spirit—our blessed soul—somehow releases itself from the physical dead body and enters into the Kingdom of Heaven providing you are good or it goes to eternal damnation in Hell if you are bad.

And what else I learned at my (then) church was that the most famous ghost, or spiritual, story was the Ascension of Jesus into Heaven—and I say this with the utmost respect to all theology and to my own faith—that Jesus' ascension into heaven is truly a remarkable, massively seen, ghost story that is written in the Bible.

We all know that Jesus died a horribly tragic and brutal death in order to pay for our sins; however, it was also to show the world at that time, and for all time to come, that when the physical body dies the spirit inside—our soul—somehow comes out of the physical body and ascends into Heaven; well, at least his did.

I'm of the opinion that it was Jesus' spirit that walked out of his tomb after three days and that his physical remains was taken away by Joseph of Arimathea and Nicodemus at both Mary's request—Mother and Magdalene—to be buried at an undisclosed location.

And even though Thomas, one of Jesus' most beloved disciples, did not at first believe it was his master who had risen from the tomb had to reach out and touch him to believe it. And when Thomas touched Jesus he knew immediately it was his dear friend, his mentor, his Lord.

Now, it is also my opinion that it was Jesus' spirit that Thomas reached out and touched, feeling the energy of what was once Jesus. And like Thomas, the majority of us are doubters of the spiritual world until we can actually, physically touch it; however, that remains so illusive even to the most ardent believers of the spiritual world.

Therefore, based on what I learned over the years of reading ghost stories that there is something inside us called a spirit, or a soul, that comes out of us when we die, like an energy release; and it is something, based on scientific research, measurable.

Our spirit is our main power source inside us. It is our energy system, like an electrical system or life-force, that runs through us which, when we die, shuts down permanently and somehow removes itself from our bodies; and then, supposedly, it goes either to Heaven or Hell.

But what if it doesn't go to either of those two places? Where does this spirit or soul go? For all practical purposes they seem to remain here, in the physical world, hiding in the dark shadows for some reason as a ghost or spirit. Supposedly we cannot see or hear them because, as some believe, they hide or reside in an area of light and sound spectrums—that we mere mortals cannot see or hear; however, dogs, cats and other animals, supposedly, can. It seems there is something beyond our human range that supposedly forbids us from seeing or hearing them; however, there are professional ghost hunters who are currently developing special equipment in hopes of exploring these unseen and inaudible spectrums so that we may learn more about where spirits, supposedly, reside or hide. Therefore, if there are spirits or ghosts that walk amongst us they, supposedly, do so in a spectrum than we can neither see or hear as disembodied energy, much like the spirit of Jesus just before his ascension into Heaven-only we, mortals, got to see his as proof of an afterlife.

Now that is a theory that intrigues me as it does any and all professional and amateur ghost hunters (and I am an amateur). And if they are disembodied energy hiding in spectrums beyond human range then it is just a matter of time before we are actually able to see beyond what we can physically perceive and communicate with the dead as if they were still with us in life.

Therefore, you may ask, have I ever seen a ghost? Do I believe in ghosts?

No, I have never seen a ghost; but I do a have a few pictures that show what are called orbs—energy spheres that are considered to be ghosts—but that in and of itself is not substantial in any way; and quite frankly it would freak me out if I did see an actual ghost, though I would like to see some other long forgotten relatives in this life before I cross over to the next one.

It seems, apparently, due to some unwritten and/or unseen law of nature we are not meant to see ghosts or spirits. There seems to be something about life's or earth's nature that forbids us to see a spirit or ghost unless we accidentally stumble onto a unexpected presence not paying attention to us stumbling mortals.

Now, as for my beliefs. As I mentioned I was taught as child that our spirit—our soul—leaves our body when we die and either goes to Heaven or Hell, meaning that we have an entity inside us that is released upon death and travels to worlds unknown to mortal man. Therefore, I believe that the soul is the spirit that becomes a ghost if it does not crossover to either Heaven or Hell, thereby becoming an entity that remains behind and haunts our known world. (I guess that is a yes.)

And this leads to another question. Why don't all souls go to Heaven or Hell if that is what they really do after leaving the body? Why are some left behind to become something that we can neither see nor hear? That is what needs to be determined. Are there really such things as ghosts roaming our world and why are they left behind to become lost spirits? Are they to bad for Heaven and to good for Hell? Or was there, or is there, another reason altogether? Who are they staying behind for? Or for what? And if we can make contact with them, what will they tell us? Do we really want to know? Should we know?

Now, having said all that, when I realized that Moonville was in my own backyard—figuratively speaking—(for I currently reside in Columbus) I had to check it out for myself—especially its haunting legends. Therefore, I went looking for it. Not just physically, but historically as well.

As I read up on the history of Moonville, from various internet sites and books, I found that many of its stories, or tales, were fractured bits of fading memories and slipping further away as time progresses and it seemed a terrible shame to let the memory of this place, this amazing little place, to disappear completely from our—Ohio's—collective consciousness. It is what inspired me to write *"An Incident at Moonville: The Conductor's Revenge"*, creating a bit of a contemporary horror-fiction, based on Moonville's haunting legends, for fun. But now I've decided to turn my notes into a straight-up book about the history of Moonville and share its many haunting legends.

Plus, there is another thing I like about Moonville, it's not your atypical haunted house or ghost town—it's a haunted tunnel. A haunted location filled with its own unique legends and lore. A haunted locale that is different from the norm and is located right here in the heart of southeastern Ohio having an ambience that no other haunted house or town can give you.

There is the rustling of leaves in the cool breezes as you seek out where the supposed ghosts might be hiding. There is the babbling of a creek as the water travels on its journey and there is the sheer fact that this little niche in the remote woods use to be a bustling little mining town that is now forevermore nevermore due to the drift of time; and that is why I decided to take the time to write down Moonville's fading history and legends.

Enjoy.

William M. Cullen

A History of Moonville

Moonville, Ohio, and its infamous tunnel, came about in the mid 1850's when the Marietta and Cincinnati Railroad (M&C RR), which originated from the 1851 consolidation of the Belpre and Cincinnati Railroad (est. in 1845) with the Franklin and Ohio Railroad, began looking for areas in southeastern Ohio to expand their westward operations and connect with Cincinnati, and other western points beyond, much faster.

Thus far, the M&C RR was only connected eastwardly with the Northwestern Virginia RR at Parkersburg, Virginia (Remember: West Virginia did not become a state until 1863) by taking a one hour, nine mile trip—for any and all cargo—by ferryboat across the Ohio River. And it only connected westward by routing trains up to Wheeling and over to Columbus in order to get a connection to Cincinnati.

In the early 1850's Cincinnati was a major shipping port on the Ohio River. It was known as the "Queen of the American West", (hence her nickname—Queen City), due, in part, to her many shipping ports. (Gambling and prostitution were other parts of Cincinnati's charms back then as well.) Cincinnati was a major docking point before heading down, or coming up from, the Mississippi River, either by St. Louis or New Orleans for any and all cargo and passenger carriers. Therefore, with Cincinnati's unique and strategic location in the Midwest it caused many an eastern railroader to want to expand their railroad fervently towards her.

Even before the rails began coming westward from such major cities as Baltimore, New York and Philadelphia and crossing the Appalachian Mountains, Ohio backers, with the same enthusiasm, were building rail lines from Cincinnati to connect eastwardly. You see, in 1850, the state of Ohio had just 575 miles of track and it was time for expanding rail lines because the country was expanding and moving westward as America's citizens began heading westward to seek out their fortunes (and misfortunes).

And one person realizing this expansive movement was the president of M&C RR—William Parker Cutler—who had the foresight to see a *"Great Central Route for the Valley of Ohio."* For it was Mr. Cutler who had the hope and determination of carrying out this massive expansion for M&C RR.

WILLIAM M. CULLEN

Mr. Cutler was born at home on July 12th, 1812 in Constitution, Washington County, Ohio just a few miles down the Ohio River from Marietta. He was the third of five children born to Ephriam and Sally (Parker) Cutler.

Ephraim (1766-1853) hailed from Edgartown, Massachusetts while Sally Parker (1777-1846) was from Newburyport, Massachusetts. They married in April of 1808 in Meigs County, Ohio.

Young William lived a typical childhood life on the family farm. He attended the local public schools with his siblings and then he, at least, went on to graduate from Ohio University in Athens, Ohio. (OU having been established in 1804, a year after Ohio entered statehood.)

As a young man Mr. Cutler pursued his interests in agriculture, but was soon encouraged to enter into Ohio politics. He was elected a member of the Ohio State House of Representatives and served from 1844-1847. He even held the position of House Speaker during his last term.

Mr. Cutler was also a trustee member of Marietta College from 1845-1889.

Mr. Cutler married Elizabeth Williamson Voris (Vores?) on November 1st, 1849. They had at least one son, Ephriam, who lived from 1858-1860.

Being a political man Mr. Cutler became a delegate to the Ohio State constitutional convention in 1850. After this Mr. Cutler became president of the Marietta & Cincinnati Railroad serving from 1850-1860; overseeing the massive RR expansion during this period for the Ohio River Valley.

In 1860, Mr. Cutler ran for and was elected as a Republican Representative to the Thirty-seventh Congress of these United States and served from March 4th, 1861-March 3, 1863, serving during the presidency of Abraham Lincoln (1809-1865). However, Mr. Cutler was unsuccessful in his re-election bid in 1862 to the Thirty-eighth Congress.

With his loss in hand Mr. Cutler came home to Marietta and resumed his interests in farming again while working for the M&C RR. Then, in 1865, Mr. Cutler assumed the position of Vice President and General Superintendent of M&C RR at a salary of $10,000 per year. (That's approximately $727,000 in 2010 inflated dollars.)

In 1865 the M&C RR was no longer a small-time operation. Their first annual report when it was filed with the Ohio Commissioner of Railroads and Telegraphs, an office created in 1867, showed that the M&C RR had 52 engines, 21 passenger cars, 580 freight cars, and employed more than 1,200 persons.

There is a rather interesting side story that involved Mr. Cutler and the M&C RR in the spring of 1865. The M&C RR ran into trouble with five rather troublesome but, yet, feisty women named the Currier sisters, who challenged M&C's efforts to build a 'shoo-fly' (a temporary track) around a hill near Athens; a line ultimately to be replaced by a tunnel.

(The M&C RR official roster lists four tunnels between Cincinnati and Athens. First, there is Byers—or The Great Tunnel—that replaced the 'shoo-fly' idea, second is Richland Tunnel—formerly Cincinnati Furnace, third is Moonville Tunnel and then fourth King's Tunnel. All are, or were, located in southeastern Ohio.)

The Currier sisters, whose names and ages were not known at the time of this writing, were apparently not all that old. I believe one of the sisters was Adeline Sidney Currier (1811-1893) whose father was Ebenezer Currier (1772-1851) of Hempstead, New Hampshire and her mother was Olive (Crippen) Currier (1786-1868) of Granville, New York. They married in Athens, Ohio in March of 1807.

Adeline Currier would have been 54 in 1865.

The Currier sisters were strong opponents to the expansion of the railroad through Athens, protesting that they didn't like the way the railroad could come in and take over land in the name of *'the greater good for the country'*. They just didn't like the idea of the excessive changes that the RR was going to bring to Athens which included congested traffic, unsavory people and in general—pollution; smoke, noise and/or otherwise. Simply put, the Currier sisters just didn't want the railroad to be built in and through Athens at all.

Therefore, the Currier sisters put M&C RR in a position to begin condemnation proceedings by doing disruptive things to the railroad, its workers and to the tracks themselves. While the proceedings were going on the sisters, to show their discontent for M&C RR and for what they felt were legal *'shenanigans'*, began tearing up a sections of tracks and began piling the rails, the ties, and the brush up in a sort of blockade on the tracks. Then, they threatened to set fire to it.

Unfortunately Mr. Cutler was not able to persuade the sisters to leave the railroad alone, therefore he had to ask the State of Ohio for assistance in resolving the Currier issue which, in the end, was taken care by legal and military means. You see, the troops were called in and the sisters were threatened with jail time, which they didn't seem to mind; however, when they were threaten with being shot for *'Acts of terrorism against the State'* they finally succumbed to the railroad's wishes and settled for *"the greater good of the country"*.

M&C RR, during Mr. Cutler's tenure as president was having serious financial issues causing Mr. Cutler to evaluate ways to cut his business expenses by looking for a more efficient route through southeastern Ohio. At the time, M&C RR, as mentioned before, had to direct the west bound cargo it received in Marietta, via the ferryboat from Parkersburg, to Wheeling by M&C trains. Being in a tough situation Mr. Cutler decided to begin offering stock subscriptions (issues of stock) in his railroad company to local southeastern Ohio landowners for rights to their lands so he could expand his railroad.

In or around 1852 or 1853 a local Athens man by the name of Samuel Coe, who happened to own some of the densest woodlands west of Athens in what is today Vinton County, heard of this stock offering and decided to take up the railroad's offer in order to allow a section of the railroad to be built on and through his land.

The original M&C RR expansion was supposed to run right through the middle of Athens with construction assistance coming from the Baltimore & Ohio RR (B&O).

Athens is built on a hill and the plan was to build a 2 percent grade up near the center of town. At that point a tunnel would be built that would run right underneath the

West State Cemetery. While the tunnel was being built, but never completed, a 'shoofly', or temporary track, was laid around the hill that resembled a big "U". After running into financial and construction problems (Currier sisters being one of them), the B&O decided to abandon the grade through town and make the shoofly permanent.

While that was going on, Samuel Coe worked to convince the railroad officials to consider another track option with him. Instead of building north of Athens and going around a place known as Hope Hollow, he would allow M&C to build through his land for free—but with one concession; which was, M&C would have to lay their tracks where he, Mr. Coe, wanted them to be, which was south of Athens. M&C carefully considered Mr. Coe's option and soon agreed to accept it. This agreement helped to save the railroad a great deal of money by reducing the amount of distance, and time, it took to get to Cincinnati.

Plus, it allowed Mr. Coe to fulfill other plans of his own.

In 1854, the U.S. Government signed a contract with M&C RR to carry mail between Cincinnati and Chillicothe, but due to the lack of funds rail-track construction was moving slowly. This slow pace prompted a local man, a man named Noah Wilson (??) to seek additional funding. (What his official position with the RR was is not known.) He headed out to seek funding in the east coast cities only to find them already inundated with debt from the railroads. Mr. Wilson's next move was to head to Europe to locate an *"angel or a saviour."* It was while he was in Paris, France that Mr. Wilson happened to meet a Polish banker by the name of Peter Zaleski (?-?). Fortunately, at that time, Mr. Zaleski was looking for good investment opportunities for his wealthy exiled Polish clients from Czarist Russia.

Mr. Wilson sold Mr. Zaleski on the 'mineral' idea of SE Ohio and Zaleski's consortium bought a million dollars worth of M&C RR second mortgages. (That's $100 million in 2010 currency.) With money in hand Noah Wilson rushed home and bought up 2000 acres of land rich in coal deposits and put it all in Mr. Zaleski's name. (Mr. Zaleski never did come to America to see what he had helped to accomplish.)

The village of Zaleski, and its locally renowned castle, are named after this generous benefactor and became the largest town in Vinton County by 1880. (In 1967 Zaleski had 1,200 residents. Today, Zaleski is home to less than 350 people.) The main shops and facilities of the RR were located in Zaleski until they burned in 1892, causing the facilities to be moved to Chillicothe.

With Mr. Zaleski's and Mr. Wilson's help Mr. Cutler and the M&C RR were able to sell enough stock subscriptions to individuals, to towns and to counties in southern Ohio that it amounted to the sum of $3 million. (That would be approximately $302 million in 2010 inflated dollars.)

A competitor, the B&O RR, had completed its main line to the Hocking River just west of Athens, in 1855. It was from here their shipments were made while waiting for the completion of a bridge across the Hocking River. Then on April 29[th,] 1856 the first railroad line finally ran directly into the city of Athens.

During 1856 and the first few months of 1857 the M&C RR built seventy-three miles eastward from its nearest Cincinnati connection in Byer, which is located in northern Jackson County, on through to Stewart Station in Athens and then turned up Big Run to run near Sharpsburg, on into Moore's Junction, then into Harmar and finally into Marietta. For many years Harmar was the end of the road until the B&O bridge was built across the Muskingum River allowing access on into Marietta.

Finally, and officially, on May 1st, 1857 M&C's railway was completed.

Even though the line came with high construction and maintenance costs it was considered a masterpiece of pioneer engineering. The rail line was now connected with the Northwestern Virginia Railroad at the Parkersburg branch with a bridge to be established later in the 1860's, after the Civil War. This also allowed the B&O RR to gain much needed access to Cincinnati and onward to St. Louis via the M&C RR line and the Ohio & Mississippi RR lines.

By the end of 1857 Mr. Cutler's expansion efforts was joined by three other groups of Ohio RR struggling for traffic between Cincinnati and the eastern seaboard.

And thus it went all through the 1850's and by the end of 1860 Ohio RR companies had laid some additional 2,371 miles of track for a grand total of 2,946 miles.

Mr. Cutler remained with M&C RR for several years and was known to have dedicated thirty years of his life to making the expansion of the railroad through Ohio River Valley a reality; however, on April 11th, 1889 Mr. Cutler died in Marietta, Ohio and is interred in Oak Grove Cemetery.

At this time it must be asked who was Samuel Coe and why did his involvement in the RR expansion figure so prominently in the development of Moonville? As mentioned, Mr. Coe owned dense forest land in west of Athens, near Lake Hope and Hope Furnace. It was on Mr. Coe's land that the town of Moonville, and three others, were established along with several train trestles and the, aforementioned, tunnels.

Samuel Coe was the the 3rd of nine children born to parents Chester Coe (b. Dec. 24th, 1784 in Granville, Hampden County, Massachusetts—d. Feb. 7th, 1849 in Zanesville, Muskingum County, Ohio,) and Roxanna (Eggleston) Coe (b. Nov 4th, 1785 in Windsor, Hartford County, Connecticut—d. Nov. 20th, 1856 in Albany, Athens County, Ohio) with them being married in Pompey, Onondaga County, New York on July 20th, 1809. Chester and Roxanna Coe lived in Connecticut and Vermont before coming to Ohio, where their remaining children were born.

Samuel was born on their fourth wedding anniversary—July 20th 1813 in Pompey, New York.

By the time Samuel was twenty-three he was courting, and eventually, married a young lady by the name of Emeline Newcomb. Emeline Newcomb was born on November 4th, 1817 in Rome, Ashtabula County, Ohio (located near Cleveland, along

Lake Erie) to parents Thomas Newcomb and Clara (Shint) Newcomb. Samuel and Emeline were married on September 4th 1836, when she was 19 years of age.

By the end of 1837 Samuel and Emeline Coe had arrived, and were living, in Rue, Athens County, Ohio having come some 200 miles south from Ashtabula County. (Rue was the official Postal Service name given to Moonville after a large tract of land in the area—the Rue Woods—which was a name given to the area by some old timers who lived in the area.) I presume, they moved to the southeastern Ohio area either in the late autumn of 1836 or in the early spring of 1837. Eventually Samuel and Emeline Coe went on to have eleven children altogether who were all born in Rue, Athens County, Ohio.

Samuel and Emeline's first child, George Delos Coe was born in Rue, Athens County, on Nov 5th, 1837. Young George grew up to become a doctor. He got married on June 17th, 1862 in Rue, Moonville, Athens County, Ohio to Mary E. McGill, (b. 1839 in Rue, Moonville, Athens County, Ohio) and moved to Missouri so he could practice medicine there. His wife Mary, unfortunately, died while they were living in Missouri on Feb. 13th, 1865 and she was buried there. When Dr. Coe decided to move back to Moonville he had his wife's body exhumed and transported back to Moonville.

Dr. Coe later remarried Laura P. Campbell (Feb 16th, 1843-?) on Oct 8th, 1874 in Rue, Moonville, Athens County, Ohio.

Frank R. Coe, (presumably a nephew) who was a *very young* boy at the time, recalled the casket arriving at the Moonville Depot. He said the casket stayed at the RR station for 2 weeks before anyone was able to move it. The body had been petrified by lime deposits back in Missouri and made it rather heavy to move. By the time they were ready to move the casket it took ten strong men to carry it.

The body of Dr. Coe's wife is said to be, possibly, re-buried somewhere south of Moonville; but how far south is not known.

As to why Samuel and Emeline Coe came to the southeastern region of Ohio in the late 1830's one can only speculate that he knew something about the area, and its potential, from someone that already knew the area; plus, it may also mean that Samuel had been through this area before.

As to that someone that already knew the area there was one Josiah Coe (March 4th, 1769-May 5th, 1843), who was born in Stratford, Connecticut. He married his first wife, Esther Curtis, (Feb. 8th, 1769-Oct. 16th, 1796) on Christmas Eve 1793, in Connecticut. Josiah was married four separate times, including Esther, and had a total of 15 children, with one of them being closely related to Samuel Coe.

In 1803 Josiah had purchased 500 acres from the Ohio Company (Northwest Territory) for $1,000.00. In 3 years time he brought his family over the mountains to Ohio from Connecticut to live at Middleton, across the Hocking River from what is now Nelsonville. While living in the area Josiah had built several mills. Also Josiah Coe was one of nine men who helped to establish the Athens Presbyterian Church in 1809.

Therefore, I presume that Josiah had let other family members know about the potential of the area causing young Samuel to come to this area to have a look around in the mid-1830's. Furthermore, I suspect, Samuel Coe well may have speculated, from his relative's findings, that he could make a potential fortune if industries were to move westward through this region. This would have certainly caused him to seek funding back home in which to buy land; and was fortunate enough to have been established in the area when, in the 1850's, M&C RR began looking for ways to expand westward through southeastern Ohio.

Therefore, it seems quite apparent, that Mr. Coe in the mid-1830's understood from his relatives claims and from his own personal experiences and education that this land was rich in minerals—clay, coal and iron ore deposits—and all he needed was a way buy it, excavate it and get it moved to the proper markets.

Knowing that the country, and the railroads were going to eventually expand westward, plus possibly suspecting that a potential war between the states was beginning to brew over slavery, may have just giving him enough foresight to stake a claim in this harsh and hilly backwoods terrain, especially along the Raccoon Creek, in the late 1830's; and possibly well into the 1850's.

The Coe's eventually owned 350 acres in what is today known as Brown Township, near what was to be Moonville. And when the M&C RR offer came along Samuel Coe was in a good position to accept it, demonstrating that Samuel Coe was an astute businessman.

Now with the M&C RR being built and coming through his property Samuel Coe was able to go forth and develop other plans such as opening more mines so he could excavate, and transport more minerals by M&C RR for bigger practical uses. With news of the expansion taking place in the area, soon more people began coming to this area searching for work in Samuel Coe's mines. The minerals that were to be mined was to be forged at nearby foundries and furnaces, usually the one at Hope Furnace approximately eleven miles west of Moonville (Hope Furnace ran along what today is Rt. 278 N of Lake Hope State Park) which operated from 1854 to 1874. Many like it were used for smelting the iron ore for making weapons for the Union Army before, during, and after the American Civil War.

With the railroad now running through his land and the mines operating at capacity Mr. Coe and his family was able to enjoy this prosperity. Having this prosperity apparently allowed Mr. Coe to dream up another plan, a plan which I believe was an unintended idea—creating his own town. (If creating your own town is not the ultimate American dream, than I don't know what is.)

This town, this dream, however was named by the railroad, not Mr. Coe. When the railroad began coming through Mr. Coe's land there was a man by the name of Moon (whether it's a surname or nickname is not known) who use to run a local general store (the local general store itself was managed, at various times, by a Mr. Dummery, a John Haney, and Frank R. Coe.) and they, the railroad, decided to put Moon's name on the town and on the nearby tunnel, not Mr. Coe's. You think it would have been Coe, Coeton, Coe's Station or Coeville, but it was not to be and that is how Moonville was officially established in 1856. Whether Mr. Coe had any say about the town's name before or after is not known.

With the railroad finally coming through there were four total towns that were created at various points near each other, with Moonville being one of them. The other three were Hope Furnace Station (or Hope Station or just Hope, which no longer exists) at the west end which was something of a shipping town, which was nearest to Hope Furnace.

Going back the other way and a mile east of Moonville, heading towards Athens, was Ingham Station a small mining town that had 25-30 houses, a general store, a school and a population that peaked at 50. (The only trace of Ingham Station today is a cellar hole and many original structures alongside the RR tracks.) Half a mile east of Ingham Station, and a mile west of Mineral (which still exists today and is two and half miles east of Moonville), where an open field is now, was the town of King's Switch.

Each town was established in either the late 1850's and/or the early 1860's; and each town had a large mine, a store and various other businesses; but it was the houses that made up the majority of each towns landscape.

Mineral, having been established before, and separately, from the other towns, had RR shipping facilities of its own as well as coal mines and a lumber business. Mineral also had a flour mill, boarding houses (one of which was ran by a widow named Mrs. Lawhead [?-?]), a school were Martie Coe (?-?) and Thomas Dellinger (?-?) were their first teachers; and a Methodist Church.

The railroad workers who traveled this region considered it to be *'the most desolate and isolated eight miles of track'*. It was known as *'the most God-forsaken stretch or rail-line from Parkersburg, W.V. to St. Louis, MO'*. Railroad workers did not like this area of the line because of its isolation and it was considered a 'dark', or without a signal, region all the way from Parkersburg to Cincinnati. And, according to the railroad workers, trains were regulated by train orders; however, other trains would show up on the line without warning—causing serious accidents.

To get to the nearest town of Hope, or Mineral, the residents of Moonville either had to walk the tracks or they bought a train ticket, if they could afford it, and rode. Riding a horse along the tracks was considered foolhardy and very rarely done because walking the tracks for an individual was considered an incredibly dangerous thing to do considering the speed at which the trains came through there—at 50 MPH. And it was considered even more of a hazard crossing the two long train-trestles in the area of Moonville and the one, or two, along the way to, or near, Mineral.

It is mentioned that Section 7, in Brown Township, was owned by Lucius Q.C. Coe. Lucius was Samuel's older brother who may have bought in on a partnership with his brother once he moved to Moonville in 1863.

Lucius Q. C. Coe was also born in Pompey, N.Y. on Dec. 15th 1811 in Pompey, Onondaga, N.Y.—died Nov 17th, 1906 in Athens County, Ohio. He was the 2nd of nine children born to Chester and Roxanna Coe.

At the age of 17, in 1828, Lucius was employed as a clerk in grocery store of Nathan Eggleston (presumably a relative). After four years, in 1832, he moved to New York City to become a salesman in a variety of stores. Lucius married Mary Jane Barbar or Barber on Oct 22nd, 1838 in NYC. It appears they had no known children.

In 1841 Lucius and Mary came to Ohio and lived on a farm in Vinton County for two years. Then in 1843 he returned to NYC where he had a mercantile business dealing with southern farmers and his business prospered.

Mary then died in 1857.

Lucius, a few years later, after the start of the Civil War, began to see his business drop off and therefore, in 1861, he sold his business interests and came back to Ohio to join his parents, his brothers and sisters in Vinton County some seven years after Samuel had started Moonville. Lucius moved to Lodi Twp where he remained for a good while.

After living in Vinton County for some time Lucius moved to Jerseyville (now Shade) in Athens County. This is where he operated a general store that had dry goods along with groceries, boots and shoes.

On September 27th, 1865 Lucius married Rebecca (Becky) H. Sanders, (May 1st, 1818 or 1828-?) a Carroll County Native, in Shade. She operated a millinery department inside the general store and they had two children—Harriet Jane and George A. Coe.

George Albert Coe b. in Jerseyville (Oct 27, 1868-March 29th, 1963) was a son of Lucius Q.C. and Rebecca Sanders Coe. George also had a sister—Harriet Jane—and a cousin named Frank R. Coe (see below). Over his formative years George attended Jerseyville schools, worked in his father's store, and took business courses at the Zanesville Business College.

When he finished school George returned to Athens to work in Harry Roach's (1860-1930 of Athens) grocery store. George also went into business and had a hardware store with a man named Frank Goldsberry (?-?). George lived in Athens County, but was interested in Vinton County. He married Bertha Williams (?-1955) in Jerseyville in 1900 and went on to have two daughters. George served as Auditor of Athens County from 1910-15 and was in insurance. He was the Secretary-Treasurer for Athens Masonic Temple for 20 years.

Frank R. Coe (Feb. 21st, 1873-?) was a Moonville farmer with 400 acres when he got married to Teeney Pinney (?-?) on October 3rd, 1900. Frank and Teeney left Moonville and moved to Saskatchewan, Canada to farm a 160 acre spread there for awhile. They retuned to Moonville in 1910 to buy and farm the Washington-Keeton Farm, with some 300 plus acres. Frank also served as the Post Office Master at his general store for Moonville for a time.

Whose Frank's parents were I have not been able to determine.

In 1868 the B&O took over the operations of the M&C RR, renaming it the B&O Southwestern.

Private investors helped to build a RR bridge across the Ohio River between Parkersburg, W.V. and Belpre; and the Little Hocking cut-off was built as well. It required about 30 miles of track, giving Washington County its first east/west main line railroad.

However, even with all this expansion, Moonville never did become a big town. Sometime in the 1870's Moonville peaked after having grown for fourteen plus years. At its peak in the 1870's and 80s, or its *'hey days'* as it has been referred to, Moonville had a population of around 100 residents (some say 50-60) and almost all of them were exclusively miners and their families. (Some of the other families that lived in the area over the years beside the Coe's were the Mace family, the Thompson family, the Dexter family, the Kennard family, the Saylor family, Ada Kennedy, Tom Fasley, Clelie James, & Mike Shea.)

Moonville, at its peak, had an inn, a saloon (or two), a sawmill down stream on Raccoon Creek, a post office, a general store, a schoolhouse that doubled as a church (the various teachers at various times were Mattie O'Neal, Mamie M. Shea, Emma Waxler, Josephine McKibben and Clelie James), a train depot as large as the one in Athens, where four trains a day stopped at Moonville, and a row of houses that were mostly for the miners and their families to live in.

The buildings were located on both sides of the tracks and all the town's people had to do was walk across them in order to get from one place to another; and, it seems, most didn't mind.

Moonville became known as a station for not only picking up and dropping off passengers, but as place to load up on lumber since the Coe brothers operated the sawmill alongside the Raccoon Creek. Plus, it was a place to pick up produce as the nearby farmers brought their goods in to market. And it was, as it was originally intended, a place to load up on minerals from the nearby mines; plus the Coe brothers kept a coal bank nearby for the trains to load up on as well, for their own use.

All this helped out the Coe's financially.

Moonville certainly bustled for such a little place out in the woods.

However, and unfortunately, Moonville's prosperity did not last very long. About thirty years, or so, after it started it began its slow demise. When Samuel Coe died in Rue, Athens, Ohio on April 21st, 1883, at the age of 69, he not only left behind his beloved wife of 46 years, he took the leadership of this small mining town with him.

However, I am sure, that Lucius Coe, Emeline Coe and family, did what they could in order to keep Moonville and its operations going for as long as possible. They would have had to since it was their livelihood.

Finally, in 1887, B&O RR bought out the complete M&C RR line. With this consolidation the east/west railroad traffic through southeastern Ohio did increase;

however, Moonville's importance began to decrease, although Moonville did continue to exist for some time to come.

It has been mentioned, and it is commonly understood by local historians, that Moonville did suffer a horrendous outbreak of smallpox in either 1890, or sometime in the 1890's. As I researched for this event through the microfilms of the Athens Messenger and Herald newspaper at Ohio University I did not find any specific articles mentioning a Smallpox outbreak for Moonville which, I presume, would have been serious big news back then if in fact it did happen considering that Moonville is less than ten miles from Athens, the largest 'city' in the area and connected to Moonville by rail line. I also mentioned the Smallpox outbreak, concerning Moonville, to the local Athens County Historical Society proprietors and they gave me the impression *it might have occurred* but any record of it would be in Vinton County records, not Athens County, since Moonville is/was in Vinton County at that time. And, as you have seen in this account, Moonville was mentioned in some birth, marriage and death records as being a part of Athens County at one time; however, apparently, by the 1890's Moonville was a part of Vinton County.

Therefore, I went back through Vinton County's microfilm for the same period and nothing seemed to be reported about this smallpox outbreak. However, I did find several medical tidbits that did occur in this period that leads me to believe that a possibility of a smallpox outbreak might have occurred, somewhere, in the area.

First, Cincinnati, like any major city of that period, had recurring outbreaks of smallpox that affected thousands of its citizens at any one time during the late 19th Century; and since smallpox is a contagious disease it is highly probable that someone, or some people, carried the contagion with them, even though they were perfectly healthy and/or semi-healthy, spreading it along the towns serviced by the railroads—much like H1N1 and air-travel in late 2009.

On Thursday, March 31st, 1892 William A. Cox dies in Mineral at the age 35 from an attack of the 'grip'. The 'grip' is a sharp sudden pain in the bowels (intestines) stemming from influenza.

Thursday, August 11th, 1892. *"A Health Movement—Complaints for some years from dwellers on the skirts of town."* This article is concerned with the unsavory and unsanitary conditions of the Hocking River by way of the Stewart Dam.

Thursday, March 22nd, 1894, Mineral—Dr. Hayes is seriously sick of lung fever.

Thursday, April 19th, 1894. Mineral—Our schools are closed for the present because of Scarlet Fever. Scarlet Fever is an acute contagious disease esp. of children, caused by Hemolytic Streptococci (strep throat) and characterized by sore throat, fever, and a scarlet rash.

Thursday, July 5th, 1894. Mineral: Dr. Coleman reports an unusual amount of sickness especially at Carbondale and Daleton.

Thursday, July 26th, 1894, *"Stamping out a pest—How Milwaukee's Health Dept. Treats Smallpox"*

Thursday, August 16th, 1894. Mineral: Dr. Coleman reports many cases of Typhoid Fever in the area. ". . . disease 'there' (has) been a result of infection." He was obviously referring to someplace locally.

Thursday, September 27, 1894, Shade: Typhoid Fever in this community (Mineral) is abating.

Sometime in 1894, an article appeared that was titled *"Smallpox Patients: How they are handled in the big city of Chicago"* Relates to what they do, or did, to handle smallpox cases in that city.

Dr. Coleman (?-?) was a physician and druggist in the area for many years. Dr. David H. Biddle (?-?) and Dr. Asher Biddle (?-?) also started practices in Mineral.

By 1895, and unfortunately for Moonville and its operations, Miss Emeline Coe died on November 5th, in Rue, Athens, Ohio having just turned the age of 78 the day before. What the children did from here I do not know but Moonville's original founders were no longer around to oversee and manage its operations.

Furthermore, by the close of the 19th Century the clay, coal and iron ore mines were both slowly being used up and closing down, or already closed down. Moonville itself was now dying from which there seemed no possibility of return.

In 1903 the Moonville Tunnel suffered a partial collapse. Repairs to the tunnel started in 1903 and were completed in 1904. There is a plaque on the far east side (down on the far right when you first come in from the west and to your left when you come in from the east) commemorating when the repairs were made and completed.

By the end of the first decade, in the new 20th Century, Moonville was all but forgotten. Just an old mining station that trains now began to pass by.

In 1919 a mining accident forced all the remaining mines to be closed causing even more demise to the Moonville community. (More about this in the next section.)

There is an abandon road, overlooking Raccoon Creek Valley, which is the location of the old school house that operated until 1920. It's gone now, but four foundation blocks still remain.

In the 1920's only one family remained in Moonville and owned farmland and they were Amza (?-May/1930's?) and Charlotte (7/7/1871-Sept. 1964) Kennard. Their granddaughter, Helen Swaim (1923?-?), and her mother, who was a Kennard, grew up in Moonville, on the north side of the track, with three sisters and a brother.

In 1930, when Helen was about seven, she returned home from school to find her home was burned to the ground after the wind blew a burning ember from a passing train—a steam locomotive. She moved in with her grandparents—the Kennards—who lived about three-quarters of a mile south of the RR tracks.

By the end of the 1930's, due to the depression mainly, Moonville had ceased to exist and all of its main buildings had been abandoned. The only things that remained were the buildings, the tunnel, the trestle supports, and the cemetery.

By 1947 Helen Swaim and her grandmother, Charlotte Kennard, left Moonville after selling their remaining farmland to the government. The last resident to leave Moonville altogether was John Thompson (?-?) in 1947. His home was bought and torn down by the state's Forestry Division for development of the area and to develop Lake Hope. Moonville was now, and completely, abandoned. Even the Coe family farmhouse had since burned down as well. (One account indicated that no one has lived in Moonville since 1991; however, they weren't sure.)

Over the next few years, even though Moonville was long gone, train traffic continued through this area. By the beginning of the 1960's, none of the buildings remained and were long gone. There was little to mark the site where Moonville stood except the town cemetery, a few foundations, the trestle supports and the tunnel.

On June 15th, 1973, the B&O merged with the Chesapeake and Ohio RR (C&O) and the Western Maryland Railroad (WM RR) to form a subsidiary of the Chessie System Express (CSX). Even though Moonville was gone, along with another town close by to the west (Hope), train traffic seemingly doubled overnight through this area with as many as 14 trains passing through each day.

By the late 1970's, the decision was made to CTC—Centralized Traffic Control the rest of the line by adding in more power operated switches, which are operated from a central location.

CSX eventually ceased operations in the Moonville area in the 1980's, abandoning the trestle supports and the tunnel. Two months after the line had been rebuilt, CSX quite using it. (While the Chessie System had been a part of the CSX Corporation since November 1st, 1980, this due to the merger of the Chessie System and Seaboard Coast Lines, it still operated as an independent railroad. But for our purposes Chessie System will be referred to as CSX going forward.)

Now check this out:

In the spring of 1981, CSX erected a B&O type railroad signal along the tracks at Moonville *because train engineers were reporting ghost sightings near the Moonville tunnel*. As of this time CSX had still not yet equipped their engines with radios and quite a few trains had gone into emergency stop *because of a ghost flagging them down*, thereby causing CSX to install a signal along the tracks in case any railroad worker in the area needed to stop a train. This signal was placed on the east side (or the Athens side) of the tunnel about 150 yards from the entrance. There was no signal for eastbound trains, just for the westbound trains. The next nearest set of signals were miles away.

CSX said that if railroad workers at Moonville needed to stop a train, they were to use this signal, not a flashlight or lantern (a good idea that was 125 years, and several lives, too late). Train engineers and conductors were ordered not to put a train into an emergency stop unless the signal was *'Red'*. All of these safety measures were put into place, specifically for this area, *because of the numerous and unpredictable ghost sightings* that had forced many trains, over the years, to go into emergency mode and stop. *And since this ghost was being reported by train operators as heading west*, it occurred to the locals, that maybe, this was the reason for the new signal.

In mid-1984, the consolidations to create CSX Transportation began. By the end of 1984 CSX had started laying down new welded rail lines. This job took up the better part of a year. By May of 1985, the whole line had been relayed. CSX had up to 10 trains running on this line, most were 'piggyback trains', but some were regular freight trains. On daily average, the line had 6 trains with more expected. The watermark, or height, of train service had been reached.

In June of 1985, CSX announced that the Saint Louis line between Cumberland and Cincinnati would be downgraded and reduced to a secondary status but still be used for east/west freight train connections. Actually all scheduled train runs between Cumberland and Cincinnati were eliminated and thereby rerouted to the Chicago line, which is about 100 miles north of Athens, adding a 480 mile detour. This change also added, anywhere, from 10 to 24 hours of travel time for freight carriers. These trains continued to run through Moonville officially until August with the last freight train running through Moonville on August 31st, 1985.

However, CSX continued running passenger trains on the decaying tracks of Moonville until the tragic death of a ten year old girl by an oncoming train in 1986. Her death caused CSX to discontinue traveling on these old rails altogether, thereby ending the use of this section of the B&O Southwestern.

Throughout 1987 CSX was working on a decision on what to do with these particular tracks. While CSX was contemplating what to do with the tracks Union Pacific (UP) or Southern Pacific (SP) had an interest in purchasing them for their own use. However, CSX took the stance of *"We don't want your offer and you can't have them"*.

Reports state that CSX put an exorbitantly high value on the line (some 10 times its value) and would not allow any new rights into Washington DC. Furthermore, CSX required all their rights on the Cumberland/Cincinnati line, including the parts they wanted to abandon, to be retained. Obviously UP, or SP, bulked at the absurdity of this.

Next CSX tried to negotiate another deal with UP, or SP, whereby they would keep the rights to the whole line and be paid a high percentage for every freight and passenger car that used the line. Plus, CSX wanted, the new owners to pay for all the maintenance costs. Essentially CSX was saying "You can't own the rail-line, but you'll have to pay to take care of it, if you use it." Obviously this absurd offer made the deal unprofitable for UP, or SP, and this deal, too, was shelved.

Having had enough of CSX's hardball tactics UP, or SP, strongly advised CSX of their plans to seek legal resolution with the Interstate Commerce Commission (ICC), thereby forcing CSX to offer a more sensible and equitable deal. But CSX had other plans and, again, seemingly overnight had started pulling track, even while they held contract negotiations. CSX pulled two sections of the line, between Cumberland and Cincinnati, with one being a thirty mile stretch into West Virginia while the other was thirty mile stretch in the direction of Moonville. It became quite apparent that CSX no longer had any use for most of the lines, but they also didn't want anyone else to use it either. They did not want other competition in area especially one that had a continental distribution which would have had other railroads rethinking their options.

Before CSX had started pulling track there were individuals that wanted to make part of the old line, through Moonville, a scenic railroad—like the one in Cass, W.V. Their idea was to buy a twenty mile section of line that ran from, what was Hope, to Mineral and put a small steam engine on the line. Funding applications were sent to the state to seek assistance in buying part of the right of way. Unfortunately, the funding did not come through and the idea was shelved; plus time had ran out since, it seemed, that CSX was in a hurry to pull the tracks.

In 1988 CSX came back to the area and began pulling up and tearing out rails lines leaving tracks on the old trestle supports that lead back to the tunnel.

Within a couple of years of the track being pulled, and with many of the trestles still intact, there was some talk of creating a bike trail starting in Zaleski State Park that would go through Hope to Moonville to Mineral and on into Athens. Several private owners bought pieces of the roadbed between Mineral and Athens which shorten the trail. Later on, the tunnel west of Mineral—King's Tunnel—was purchased and added to the trail.

Zaleski State Park sent in a request for funds to the state as they negotiated with CSX for purchase of more roadbeds. CSX trashed that deal by having the all the trestles removed knowing that Zaleski State Park would have needed them if they wanted to make their trail. The rumor was that UP, or SP, wanted to buy the line if the ICC would help them negotiate a fair deal with CSX. So what CSX did was to start pulling all the bridges, including some very long truss bridges, along with thirty more miles of track from Athens eastward to within 10 miles west of Parkersburg.

With the state finding this out they realized they did not enough money to rebuild the bridges for the park nearly killing the hope of a bike trail. But the idea of a trail still remains a very popular one in the area and is even still being promoted by the good people of the Moonville Rail Trail Association to this very day. (Please see moonvillerailtrail.com to learn more.) Therefore, for now, plans to make an exciting bike trail have not (yet) been realized, or died.

Sometime in the early 1990's CSX came back again and pulled the remaining tracks they left behind on the trestle supports, leaving behind the wood beams and a gravel path to the tunnel, which was left standing.

After the line was abandoned, the tunnel was supposedly listed as an Ohio Historic Landmark; however, I have not been able to locate it on any Historic Landmark listing. And it should be because it is the only brick tunnel in the Southeastern part of the state, and of course, marked the place where Moonville once stood.

Then a rumor spread in the 1990's that CSX had dynamited the tunnel. This proved (thankfully) not to be true. CSX did plan to dynamite the tunnel, but, fortunately, changed their minds. As far as anyone knows CSX could still make it a real possibility and destroy the tunnel. But, for now, no plans have been made to destroy the tunnel, though it is in need of renovations before time destroys it.

CSX's decision not to destroy the tunnel came right after the other tunnel, King's Tunnel, was purchased by a couple of brothers for growing mushrooms and the line through Athens was pulled. It appears CSX may have calculated the cost to rebuild new lines as being too expensive, thereby destroying the tunnel would not be necessary.

Towards the end of the 20th Century, or sometime very early into the 21st Century, CSX came back again and finally removed the old wood beams that crossed the old trestle supports. By doing this they made the only way possible to get to Moonville Tunnel by having to cross over, or wade through, Raccoon Creek and climbing up the hill to the other side, where the tunnel is located. Meaning, it appears, that CSX's main reason for removing the tracks was due to insurance liability. No reason for being sued by some careless person for tripping over tracks or falling off a trestle support. Fortunately, CSX left the old brick tunnel to stand.

The brothers that bought King's Tunnel learned that the tunnel did make a great place to grow mushrooms. In fact, their business did so well that they considered buying Moonville Tunnel for future expansion. However, there was an issue. With the trestle crossings pulled up, Moonville Tunnel becomes impossible to reach when Raccoon Creek rises due to rains; which means, the trestles needs to be rebuilt and that proved to be a an expensive business proposition and thus, a deterrent to their plans.

There was a person who owned a majority of the abandoned RR property that wanted to make sure the public was in favor of the idea of having a bike trail before moving forward with the project. This majority landowner seemed pleased with the results of a turnout where 115 crowded the main room at Lake Hope State Park Lodge not to long ago. The general feeling is that it will happen one day.

Last known the majority owner has yet to decide whether to sell or donate the abandoned right-of-way.

Today, the Moonville Tunnel has been in existence for 150 plus years and the area still, so far, remains accessible. Also the tunnel remains (so far) as a living memorial and is in need of dire repair if we wish to retain the memory of a bygone era. The memory is brought on by what remains: the tunnel, the trestle supports, and the foundations of old buildings and the cemetery of its former residents.

In fact some members of the Coe family are buried in that cemetery. One is a Union soldier named Wellington Coe (?-?) who was a member of Co. C 30 Ohio Infantry. In one web photo there is, supposedly, a Union soldier standing in the nearby tree line. The question is, is it the spirit of Wellington Coe or just a good photo-shop image? Also, there is a Cliff Coe (1844-1899) and Lovisa Coe (1843-1883) buried there and what relation they are to any of the other Coe's is not known.

Now, primarily, it is the tunnel, with its colorful history, that still brings out the curiosity seekers to see this area—just check out all the various websites and YouTube videos dedicated to its memory. This nearly forgotten tunnel is one of the few remaining items that are left of a small mining town that thrived for a very short time in Ohio historically speaking.

To give you an idea about the tunnel it is approximately 500 yards to the east of where Moonville was, across a now abandoned train trestle support that went over Raccoon Creek. The tunnel itself is fifty yards long and has a slight curve built into it. It is very narrow by railway standards where trains would speed through at full throttle giving very little, if any, clearance on either side.

The tunnel was originally built of sandstone and as mentioned was repaired with bricks and mortar in 1903-04 that are now falling apart. Inside the tunnel it is covered in black soot from former engine smoke and makeshift fires of dwellers; plus, it has some rather pitiful graffiti that it doesn't deserve to be there. The outside is covered in more pitiful graffiti that it doesn't deserve; plus, there is the ever encroaching forest.

Moonville Tunnel needs to be treated more like a registered Ohio landmark than a forgotten relic of a bygone era. The state of Ohio should and could preserve it even more, as an historical landmark, before it falls down.

I say we, fellow Ohioans, should preserve it and find a way to connect it with the beauty of Lake Hope via a Scenic Railway and/or bike trail; and there is an organization out there right now trying to do just that.

As I mentioned earlier there is a group called the Moonville Rail Trail Association (MRTA) (moonvillerailtrail.com) located in Hope, Ohio. They hold monthly meetings on how best to obtain financing to preserve this significant landmark and create their trail.

I have personally met the people of this wonderful organization who meet in an authentic, well-preserved, one-room school house in Hope, and they are a determined in making this trail a reality.

MRTA was established in 2001 and currently consists of at least 55 individuals and/or family members, along with 6 organizations. MRTA has secured grants to purchase land needed to convert the abandon B&O RR right-of-way into a multi use recreational trail that will traverse parts of Vinton and Athens County. They are currently working on putting together a 16 mile trail running from Red Diamond in Vinton County to Grosvenor in Athens County, along primarily old railroad bed lines.

The goal of MRTA is to connect the Moonville Rail Trail to Hocking Adena Bikeway in Athens. Phase One being from Red Diamond to Hope School Interpretive Center. Phase Two is from Hope School Interpretive Center to Mineral, passing through the Moonville Tunnel. Phase three is from Mineral to Grosvenor in Athens; and Phase Four is from Mineral to Carbondale.

Finally, I highly recommend to anyone, especially to all you trail-riders, hikers and nature buffs that are interested in learning more about MRTA and their project to contact them, or to contact the Dept. of Natural Resources of Ohio. (dnr.state.oh.us/parks/lake hope).

A Collection of Moonville's Haunting Tales

It's not only the historical and the physical aspects of the tunnel that draws visitors out to see it. The other draw is its very mysterious and haunting history that causes people, from all around the region, to travel all the way out to the deep backwoods of Vinton County to see this tunnel. People that have gone out there say they have had odd or unexplainable experiences such as camera flashes not working while standing in the middle of the tunnel. (As I have mentioned before this has happened on several different occasions to more than one person.) Or they get pictures that have anywhere from one to several orbs in them. Orbs are said to be energies of spirits and that they come in various colors, shapes and sizes in appearances.

Some say they hear water trickling inside the tunnel, but the ground remains dry.

Supposedly you can hear a little girl's laugh as you walk into the tunnel. Maybe that is the laugh of the 10 year old girl that was killed out there?

Some say the scent of stale lavender is still known to be present in the area long after a woman was run down by a speeding train.

Others say they have seen a lantern floating in the air, with no possible means of support.

And as I mentioned before, there are some hearty railroad workers have been known to see a ghost standing alongside the tracks as they came traveling through. But whose ghost is it?

Therefore, what are all these mysterious and haunting stories that surround Moonville?

I'll do my best to explain.

Based on the research I have gathered there are at least sixteen known deaths out at Moonville, as well as some other interesting incidents. In this harsh wooded environment and over several decades since Moonville started, it is given fact that many have died out there for various reasons. But, I presume, there are a lot more than we know about. Let's take a look at what has been determined over the years.

Much of what is known about the Moonville ghost, or ghosts, comes from the recollections of Michael L. Shea and George Tolliver.

A HISTORY OF MOONVILLE, OHIO AND A COLLECTION OF ITS HAUNTING TALES

In 1967 Michael "Mike" L. Shea, (August 17th, 1891-Jan 1969) was a former superintendent of one of the clay mines at Moonville. It was Mike's ancestor, Timothy Shea, who came from Ireland to get away from the potato blight and start a new life in this region. Mike was a resident of McArthur, Ohio who had worked in Moonville, and was persuaded by his niece, Frances M. Williams of Zaleski, to record his recollections of Moonville. (And for those of you that know, Shea Road is named for Mike's family.)

As a boy George Tolliver (March 2nd, 1903-March 1973) lived and grew up at Ingham Station. Paraphrasing his story from 1970, some sixty years before, as a boy, George Tolliver was very nearly killed by, and narrowly escaped, a fast moving train while out on the Moonville train-trestle. *"Between Mineral and Moonville there are two tunnels and four trestles on a stretch of railroad and no other way to get between Mineral and Moonville but to cross the railroad and its trestles. The people use to walk the tracks between the two towns all the time. The trains ran full speed—50 mph—over that area and if you happened to be caught in the tunnel, or on a trestle, that was your last trip. There have been many persons killed on that short piece of RR."*

Mr. Tolliver tells of a legendary, disembodied soul, (from his account in 1970) who more than a half century before caused train wrecks and the death of a train-man near the Vinton and Athens County line. Mr. Tolliver stated that two Dexters (Erastus and possibly a brother) were killed on the tracks, both at different times. Mr. Tolliver would not say for fact that the ghost of Moonville was Bub Dexter, but he did say that (paraphrasing) *"It is a colored man of about eight feet tall, walking like he was on stilts, wearing a miner's cap and oil lamp on his head, having flame flowing over his shoulders was said to come down the tracks. He had been seen many times between Mineral and Moonville and some say he can still be seen on moonless nights."*

Along with these two men's accounts and various other resources these are the following accounts of what has happened in the area around Moonville, its trestles, and its tunnel.

WILLIAM M. CULLEN

The Falling Brakemen

According to the Ohio Exploration Society (OES), The McArthur Democrat and other documented sources, the most popular, and familiar story, in relationship to the tunnel is what happened in the late 1850s, when a brakeman was crushed under the wheel of a moving train. The legend is based on historical fact but after years of being retold it has become quite distorted. The story is that *someone* was crushed under the wheels of a moving train that used to go through the Moonville Tunnel. Apart from that the story gets clouded. Plus, there have been so many other brakemen, or railroad employees, that have been killed under the wheels of trains in this area who had carried lanterns that the cloud may never lift on the story.

First a brakeman's job was known to be a very dangerous position in those early days of steam engine trains. The brakeman's job consisted of connecting and disconnecting the train cars, operating the brakes on a train either between the cars, or on top of the cars, depending on the cargo; plus, being an overall assistant to the train's conductor. And in those early days of steam locomotives it took 4 hours to fire up a steam engine and two hours to check lubrication; including coal and water supplies.

During that period all train-cars were equipped with the link-and-pin coupler system used to fasten one car to another and were very hazardous to the life of a brakeman. The train cars each had long iron links, like a chain link, that a brakeman had to "pin" together with a large iron pin in order to get the cars connected. The brakeman's job was to stand between the two oncoming cars (boxcars or freight cars) that were being pushed down the track by yardmen or other brakemen, while the train-cars were in either a train-yard or on a side track that connects to a main track at a remote location, so that the brakeman could link-and-pin them together. Typically the brakeman usually had only one chance to get the pin in between the two links, at just the right moment, or face being crushed to death by the two cars crashing together. (Auto couplers and air brakes did not appear until the 1870's and 1880's respectively.)

The second part of a brakeman's job consisted of slowing down or stopping a fast moving train. Say that an engineer wanted, or needed, to slow down a steam train in order to pick up, or drop off, a supply load, he would have to blow a certain train whistle signal that would cause the brakemen to start running from car to car, setting the hand brakes.

The handbrakes on a passenger train-car are manual brakes that are mounted on the outside of the train-car just beyond the passenger door. These brakes were located in such a way that they were near the connecting link-and-pin couplers that just happen to be above were the wheels are located. With one good solid jolt from the train, while turning the brake-wheel, a brakeman could lose his grip and fall off getting seriously injured and/or killed. It is commonly known that many brakemen had a bad habit of falling off a moving train and landing in between the train-cars while they were doing their work.

Freight cars were even worse. The manual handbrake wheel was located not at the passenger level but on top of the roof of the train-car and proved to be much more dangerous. The brakemen had to go outside the freight car, climb up a ladder that was on the end of the car, or on side of the car, and try to work, turning the brake wheel, on top of moving, shifting trains. Furthermore, many a brakemen fell to his death on a stormy winter night trying to walk the icy treacherous 'running boards' that are on top of these freight cars going from one handbrake wheel to another.

Often, for both types of cars, in the very poor weather conditions of winter and the early spring, this was very dangerous work. And, to compound the situation, if it was cold out, such as a train moving at thirty miles an hour in 30 degree temperatures that creates a wind-chill of 15 degrees, so you can just imagine if it was colder and they were moving faster. Therefore, these men would often carry their own bottles of whisky and have a few drinks in order to keep warm while outside.

Now a couple of stories tell of a M&C *railroad worker* (what position is not known) who had been resting and drinking heavily one night while sitting on a boxcar that sat on a side track. After the boxcar had been coupled and the train pulled out, the railroad worker decided to ride the train to the next stop by hanging onto the outside of the boxcar. He, apparently, slipped and fell off the train just outside one of the two tunnels (as mentioned there is King's Tunnel located a few miles down the track from Moonville's Tunnel) landing in such a way that he was hit by the train and his body fell in such a way that his head was ran over by a wheel and was decapitated.

People, today, who claim to see this ghost say that he is always wearing his railroad uniform, walking along the tracks, carrying a lantern with him. And they also claim that the ghost is headless.

Or was it the *flagman* at the Moonville depot who had become very drunk while resting and when he heard the train, he picked up his lantern in a pointless attempt to flag down the train. While standing on the tracks, waving his lantern and arms, he had just appeared into the train's light when he was run over by the steam locomotive and killed.

Supposedly, when you come on a moonless night and wait for an eastbound train you'll see a flagman waving a lantern trying to get the train to stop.

No dates are given for these stories so they could have happened almost anytime, to anyone, in the history of the railroad line along this track.

Most of these types of stories are based on the following newspaper article that appears in the McArthur (Ohio) *Democrat* dated Thursday, March 31st, 1859:

> "A brakesman on the Marietta & Cincinnati Railroad fell from the cars near Cincinnati Furnace, on last Tuesday, March 29, 1859 and was fatally injured, when the wheels passing over and grinding to a shapeless mass the greater

part of one of his legs. He was taken on the train to Hamden and Doctors Wolf and Rannells sent for to perform amputation, but the prostration of the vital energies was too great to attempt it. The man is probably dead ere this. The accident resulted from a too free use of liquor."

As you can tell the article does not say who the brakeman was, his race, or anything about him except his position—*a brakesman*. Hence, there are a couple variations to this story based on this article. One variation is that some time in 1859, after stopping in Moonville on a supply run, a *brakeman* for M&C RR had been passing his break time with a bottle of liquor in one hand and his lantern in the other. Either from exhaustion or drunkenness, or both, the brakeman fell asleep. Sometime during the night he was awaken by the sound of his train leaving the Moonville depot. He tried to get up to quickly, rising up rather wearily, thereby stumbling onto the track and falling beneath the wheels of the moving train. The brakeman was not killed instantly but he never recovered from his injuries, soon dying from them. It is said that his ghost can be seen stumbling down the tracks, inside the tunnel with his lantern in hand, still trying to catch the train before it leaves Moonville Station.

The other variation is that the ghost that is most often seen at the Moonville Tunnel is the ghost of an *eight-foot tall African-American Negro who was a brakeman.* Some time in the late 1850's there was, supposedly, an eight-foot tall African-American Negro who was a brakeman on the M&C rail line. Many think this is Erastus Dexter. But it is not. (More about him later.) I'm sure this man was just another hardworking, quite probably a free, black male, who was a rather tall brakeman who had heard the whistle signaling to stop the train. And before hopping outside to work on a moving freight train car, he may have taken a good long swig of whiskey in order to keep warm from the constant on-rushing cold wind of a very early Ohio spring season, just like any other brakeman.

Furthermore, this brakeman, most likely, was working on top of a freight car as they traveled down the tracks and because of his extraordinary height and size may have been struck by a tunnel entrance before he was able to quickly duck down and get out of the way; therefore, being violently shoved off the top of the car as it went through the tunnel. This caused the brakeman to fall off the train but land in such a way that he was able to grasp a cable and be dragged along the tracks while having one of his legs crushed by the train's 5 inch wide rapidly spinning wheels before being discovered near Cincinnati Furnace.

By the time the conductor had been able to get to the engineer and have him grind the train to a screeching halt one of brakeman's legs was turned into a 'shapeless mass' mangled by the wheel causing extensive bleeding and bone damage. This brakeman was then rushed to a nearby train station, in Hamden, Ohio, which is still located nine to ten miles south of McArthur in south-central Vinton County, and is no where near Moonville Tunnel, where Doctors Wolf and Rannells were sent for in order to perform an amputation. And as you read their diagnosis determined that the *'prostration of the vital energies was too great to attempt it. This brakeman probably died 'ere of this'.*

The accident resulted, per the doctors, from *'a too free use of liquor'* making this the story that appears in the McArthur Democrat on Thursday, March 31st, 1859 with the only exception being is that we don't know the true race of the victim. Therefore, this story should not even be associated with Moonville in any way, shape, or form except to say that it shared the same rail line that went through Moonville, some nine to ten miles to the north of Hamden.

Having said that, the loud shrieks of agony and pain of a man screaming, that are said to be heard in the tunnel from time to time, maybe attributed to this agonizing brakeman; however, it is very unlikely.

I'll soon explain why.

Either way all we can be sure of when it comes to this legend that in the late 1850's, on Tuesday, March 29th, 1859, that some man, either black or white, while drunk, and carrying a lantern, fell off or got knocked off a train and had one of their legs crushed; eventually dying from it.

How tragic.

A couple of versions have different locations as to where the brakeman was before he was killed. One version has it that a *brakeman* got drunk while playing cards with some others at the, or one of the, *local saloon(s)*. On his way back to wherever he was going he had to walk through the tunnel. As he was going through a train was coming and he attempted to stop the train by swinging his lantern back and forth. This, unfortunately, didn't work and he was hit by the train and decapitated. It is said that his ghost is now haunting the tunnel, swinging his lantern back and forth for eternity. But this story also goes along with another story except replace the brakeman with a miner.

The other version is that one rainy night a *brakeman* was getting drunk while playing cards with some fellow workers in a *shanty* near the tracks. He got up and staggered outside (I think he went to relieve himself in the nearby woods). While doing whatever it was that he was doing he swayed into the path of an oncoming steam locomotive and was killed when that B&O train ran him over. This, supposedly, happened near the turn of the century. The others were still inside playing cards and they didn't even miss him. The brakeman was found the next morning along the railroad tracks. He was supposedly buried in Moonville cemetery.

Supposedly on a rainy night near the tunnel you'll see the brakeman with a red lantern *'a glimmerin and a waving'*. It is said that each night a railroad man use to stand along the tracks, with his lantern, to signal the train.

One morning a man was found lying, bloodless, along the tracks. There were no clues as to why he was dead. Now, it was not made known as to what they account meant by 'bloodless'. Was the body void of blood as if someone or something drained his blood? Or did they mean that there was simply no blood around the body, indicating that he wasn't struck by a train, which instantly causes blood to splatter from a body like water from a busted water-balloon; therefore, meaning that the man may have either died from natural causes or by some other mysterious means.

As you can tell there are many variations on the railroad worker, brakeman, or flagman stories. The only thing that is true that some railroad individuals over the many years of this rail-line being in use were killed in horrible accidents; such as the stories of Alfred Simpson and Tim Shannong.

On May 20th, 1886 Alfred Simpson, age 23, (1863-1886), a brakesman, was pulling a pin at Hamden in Vinton County one Sunday evening when he got his foot caught in a 'frog'. A frog is a device on railroad track for keeping cars on the proper rails at intersections or switches. Before Mr. Simpson could get himself freed the engine that was approaching could not be stopped in time and ran him over, mangling the lower part of his body.

Tim Shannong (?-?), a brakeman, slipped and fell off of a car and was killed on the Carbondale branch. Carbondale is a few miles north of the Mineral/Moonville line.

It was not surprising to learn that during the Civil War engineers used to hang two red lanterns beneath their locomotive's headlights knowing that both northern and southern forces respected those symbols as being couriers of mercy—a hospital train; and any engineer wanting to protect his train and its shipments learned to use this method. However, it has been said that anyone visiting the area should be ever so vigilant of seeing such dangling red lanterns, for they indicate ghost-trains, trains that are known to carry the spirits of dead soldiers.

An M&C RR Marker summary on the line between Mineral and Moonville: *"A red lantern* (seen hanging) *in a tree suggests the annual passage of the ghost* (trains) *of this short tunnel."*

One final note about the brakemen of Moonville is that there is a bluegrass gospel band by the name of *Rarely Herd* who wrote a song based on these legends, entitled *"Moonville Brakeman"*.

(As of this writing there were no videos of this song on YouTube, however The Ohio Exploration Society has a copy of it on their website under Structures—Moonville Tunnel; plus the band has its own website. The song is classic Bluegrass and well worth hearing.)

A Miner

A young man by the name of Raymond Burritt (1901-1919?), who was an 18-year-old miner, was killed in a Moonville mining accident in 1919. Raymond had set off a charge of dynamite in order to loosen up the coal for easier digging and hauling. But, after the dynamite went off, he returned to the mine too soon and was caught, and crushed, in an avalanche of coal. The coal mines were abandoned and closed after this incident, having a dire affect on the community of Moonville as mentioned before.

At nearby Hope Furnace it has been said that there is an apparition of a night watchman that can be seen carrying his lighted coal oil lantern while pacing back and forth on top of the restored furnace. Part of his duty was to walk the tipple, or top, of the furnace, with his lantern, to make sure all was secure. While out doing his duty one dark and rainy night he was momentarily blinded by a flash of lightening, supposedly around 8 PM, that caused him to slip and fall into molten bowels of the furnace and be burned to death. No date is given as to when this happened.

There is a place called Lookout Rock at Moonville. One night 20 men, presumably miners and railroad workers, were treed by wolves for the entire night. They had to taken refuge at Lookout Rock in order to get away from the wolves. So while they waited for the wolves to go away they bravely, somehow, snuck down from out of the trees and built a fire, keeping it going all night on Lookout Rock.

The citizens of Moonville could see the fire burn throughout the night and the sound of nearby baying wolves.

No date was ever given as to when this happened.

Small Pox and the Brave Volunteer

At one time, presumably in late 1893 or early 1894, Moonville was struck and ravaged by an epidemic of smallpox, forcing the whole town to be quarantined.

Smallpox, as you may know, is a very contagious and deadly infection caused by the variola virus which is a pustle, pimple, or blister that has pustular eruptions, or pus. It can be passed from one person to another through coughing, sneezing, or breathing, or by contact with the scabs or the fluid from blisters. It can even spread from an infected person's personal items and bedding.

The first symptoms, or signs, of smallpox are a severe illness that causes a high fever, fatigue, a headache, and a backache. It takes about 12 days for these symptoms to manifest and appear once infected. After about another 2-3 days a red-blotchy rash will appear on the body. The rash usually starts on the face and upper arms, and eventually spreads all over the body. Smallpox is easiest to spread during the first week of the rash.

(A severe chickenpox rash can be mistaken for a smallpox rash at first. But different viruses cause these illnesses.)

Then over the next 2 to 3 weeks, the flat, red spots become firm and dome-shaped and fill with pus. Eventually they scab over and the scabs will fall off after 3 to 4 weeks once the rash first appears, leaving behind pitted scars. As scabs form, the person becomes less contagious. But a person can spread the virus from the time the rash first appears until all scabs have fallen off.

If a smallpox outbreak occurred and had been confirmed by a simple examination of the rash, and a few simple questions about the symptoms, a doctor would've considered it a health emergency. He, or she, would've had to take quick action. They would've had to keep anyone who might have been exposed away from others. It was absolutely vital to keep people away from anyone that were infected. An infected person would've been quarantined from all other people until they were no longer contagious to help prevent it from spreading. Thus, in Moonville's case, the whole town became quarantined.

Back before there was a vaccine (which today is no longer used since it was known to have killed people), smallpox use to cause serious illness and many deaths all around the world. Today there is no known cure for smallpox. Treatment includes drinking plenty of fluids and taking medicines to control pain and fever. Today, smallpox is contained in various labs throughout the world for research (hopefully looking for a cure).

With the quarantine in place trains were ordered not to stop at Moonville—not for any reason—due to the highly contagious disease. Soon the residents of Moonville were running low on supplies of all kinds and were subsequently starving and dying; thereby, needing to come up with a way to get the trains to stop and deliver its supplies to them.

Therefore, the citizens of Moonville called a meeting and got together in order to come up with a plan whereby they should send one of their own out and through the tunnel to the other side, to the outskirts of their town, with a lantern to signal for a train to stop. As the train would approach the man with the lantern would then signal for help, waving his lantern. Since he would be standing outside of the town's limits, it was thought, that the train conductor would stop the train in order to help this man.

This they agreed upon doing.

A volunteer was soon selected and it was said to have been a local doctor who was low on medical supplies. (Was this, possibly, Dr. George Delos Coe? It would make perfect sense since he was living in Moonville at the time and a valuable community leader since having been born in Moonville.) And since doctors are known to wear white coats, jackets or smocks to indicate their profession it would make sense for him to wear his white coat, indicating who he was. Plus, it was said, that the volunteer was an older, white bearded man who, apparently, was more than fifty years of age (Dr. Coe was 56 in 1893) and on the very next morning he started out for the tunnel, carrying a yellow lantern.

He would've walked the 500 yards, crossing over the train-trestle that crossed over Raccoon Creek, heading eastward. At the moment he was going through the tunnel he heard a train was coming. The man knew that the conductor of the train would not stop unless he was on the other side of the tunnel, just outside of the town's limits. So the man took off running, through the tunnel, as fast as he could, waving his yellow lantern.

He was apparently sick and delirious from the small pox himself and was staggering in front of the oncoming train, while frantically waving his lit lantern through the darkness of the tunnel, trying to alert the train of his presence. With the train quickly chugging towards him, and the tunnel, the man was not seen by the train's engineer, who had steam and smoke billowing all around him as he blew his warning whistle, as he approached the train near the tunnel, and thus was not able to see the man and stop in time.

And since the running volunteer was not able to make it all the way through the tunnel in time was then struck down by the speeding train and instantly killed, supposedly by being decapitated.

With his death many of Moonville's inhabitants supposedly succumbed to the small pox by either dying of the disease or simply through starvation with only a few surviving the whole ordeal. Thus, with his death, it is believed that this brave and noble volunteer became the Moonville Ghost with its flowing white beard and blazing red eyes that look like balls of fire who disappears into the nearby rocks whenever a train approaches.

(Use to anyways.)

Or, as some believe, and it was quite possible, that Moonville was burned down to the ground by an overly frightened and fanatical mob with all its diseased inhabitants.

Those that couldn't make it out of their properties alive were burned to death while those that did get out a live sought refuge in the nearby woods. Those that made it to the woods may have eventually succumbed to the elements of the environment by either freezing to death or starving. Also it is quite possible that many of the infected were shot dead by local men acting as snipers, waiting in the lurch; thereby, wiping out a whole town of innocent men, women and children for being unfortunate enough in contracting the smallpox virus.

Therefore, if it happened at all, this smallpox incident on Moonville was most certainly a tragic catastrophe.

Some say, that this story is based purely on myth and never occurred and that may have some merit. Unless, of course, and I speculate, that Moonville's outbreak, which may have occurred in late 1893 or early 1894, wasn't supposed to have been reported or it was considered too insignificant to make the news and history books.

After reviewing newspapers and historical books, located at the Ohio University Alden Library, the Worthington (Ohio) Public Library, and the Vinton County Westcot Library in McArthur, there are no records (thus far) to support a smallpox outbreak of ever happening at Moonville; but that doesn't mean that it didn't happen. In fact, Ohio had several smallpox outbreaks throughout this state in the 19th Century, with Cincinnati being hardest hit. And, as you may recall, the railroad line that ran through Moonville was created in order to find a faster route to and from Cincinnati. And with Cincinnati's population being in the thousands its smallpox outbreaks would have been considered far more significant to report statewide than a place like Moonville; whose population of 50 to 100 residents would not have been considered significant news to the larger world; but it would have been to the dying and starving people of Moonville.

WILLIAM M. CULLEN

The Headless Conductor

There is a ghost story dating from as far back as the 1890's. It is, supposedly, one ghost where there have been many sightings of this ghost over the years that looks like a headless conductor, carrying a red and green lantern, searching the tracks of Moonville tunnel for his severed head. It is believed that this ghost's story is based on some loose facts of a seemingly benevolent B&O conductor who had asked, or ordered, the train's engineer to stop at Moonville one day, while the small pox epidemic was still going on, in order to leave behind some supplies. It has been rumored that this conductor had made more than a few trains stop near the Moonville tunnel, for various reasons.

The engineer, at first, didn't want to break the railroad's policy of not stopping at Moonville during this epidemic. But with the conductor's much assisting the engineer finally, and grudgingly, agreed to stop the train and they just happened to stop part of the train just inside the tunnel. This allowed the conductor to drop off some much needed supplies to the quarantined residents of Moonville.

While being stopped the engineer, had asked or ordered, the conductor to get under a freight car, with the pretext of inspecting it for a leak in the brake line. Reluctantly, the conductor, with his lantern in hand, got under a freight car with the intent of assisting the engineer. While the conductor was getting under the freight car the engineer apparently walked back up to the engine compartment.

Now, it was a known fact that the engineer and the conductor did not get along.

Some accounts say it was a brakeman that ordered the conductor under the car. But knowing that the brakeman's position was to assist the conductor and thereby would not be in a position to make such an order it would then seem more appropriate to believe that the engineer was doing the asking, or ordering, of the conductor—thus being our main culprit.

With the conductor under the freight car on the premise of inspecting the brake line the engineer, supposedly, *'goosed the throttle'*, jerking the train forward with the intent of knocking over the conductor. When the conductor's head landed on the rail the engineer kept the train moving forward causing the conductor to be decapitated by the train's revolving 5 inch wide wheels, thereby severing the head from its body.

It appears the engineer then stopped the train, got out, went over and grabbed the head and threw it into the nearby woods causing the ghost of the conductor to go and look for it. Some people say they've seen a light from what looks like a lantern *'bobbing around'* in the woods supposedly looking for a severed head. And, supposedly, when the conductor does find his head the engineer (and possibly his descendants) will have a day of reckoning, if they should ever come to Moonville.

Apparently at some point in time the engineer, being insanely jealous, had either found out, or had a very strong belief, that the conductor was having an affair with his wife and saw an opportunity to extract his revenge by having the conductor run over. Therefore, an enraged engineer, supposedly not prone to violence, waited for an opportune moment—thereby showing intent. What the engineer did with the body and head after that is not really known, but it appears he made have played it off as an accident.

It has been said that a park ranger in the 1960's or 70's came up with this story of a bed-hopping conductor and a jealous engineer to give a *"bit of spice"* to an old ghost story; but on the other hand, there was an eyewitness.

One day the engineer told the crew to load up so they could leave. As they went down the tracks, the crew noticed that the conductor wasn't on board. They went back to Moonville in case the conductor had missed the train. When they didn't find him in town they decided to go back up the track to see if he had fallen off the train. Just as the engineer gave the train some steam the bloody head of the conductor fell in through the front window. They all scrambled out to investigate but couldn't find any sign of the body; or blood.

The crew questioned everyone in Moonville. One old man said *he saw* that the engineer had *'asked'* the conductor to check something under the front of the train. As soon as he had crawled underneath the engineer told the men it was time to pull out. So the engineer caused the conductor's death, *says the old man*. The conductor now, supposedly, carries a red and green lantern while some have even heard his screams at night.

Unfortunately, who this old man was is not known.

Another theory says that the conductor was having an affair with the brakeman's wife and he was pushed out of the train and ran over. Maybe this is a separate incident altogether.

Another account of the conductor's death is published in a magazine called *"Highways"* (October 1990, vol. 24, no. 10.). In this version the train was pulling out of the Moonville station and began gathering steam. While moving along the bloody head of the conductor supposedly rolled down from the roof and fell down *past* the engineer's window. Seeing this, the engineer brought the train to an emergency stop. The engineer quickly ordered the crew to search for the body, and head, of the conductor. After an extensive search no body, or head, was ever found. Nor was there ever any blood found along the tracks to indicate that the conductor was killed on the tracks. He seemed to have vanished in the night, into the rocks nearby.

Another version is that a train conductor, like the brakeman, was drunk and fell in front of the train car and was decapitated.

One version described the ghost as being a 'dark' male figure who is dressed as a conductor and swings a lantern while standing inside the Moonville tunnel. He is described as wearing a miner's hat, thus confusing people as to whether he is a miner or a railroad worker. This, I believe, is a whole other person; and I'll get to that person shortly.

One account claims a B&O engineer reported seeing a man, who was dressed as a conductor of the M&C RR swinging his lantern back and forth, inside the tunnel. As the train came to a stop the engineer noticed that the man was headless as he walked away from and off of the tracks, disappearing somewhere into the rocks nearby. Apparently, this appearance was a few years before the man wearing a miners hat was killed in the tunnel.

Back on Sunday, February 17th, 1895 the Chillicothe Gazette reported that the, or a, Moonville ghost was once again appearing in front of a fast moving train and then disappearing into the rocks after the train had stopped. The article is:

> *"The ghost of Moonville, after an absence of one year, has returned and it is again at its old pranks, haunting B&O S-W freight trains and their crews. It appeared Monday night, February 11th, in front of fast freight No. 99 west bound, just east of the cut which is one half mile the other side of Moonville at the point where Engineer Lawhead lost his life and Engineer Walters was injured.* (I wonder what happened to these two men?) *The ghost, attired in a pure white robe, carried a lantern. It had a flowing white beard, its eyes glistened like balls of fire and surrounding it was a halo of twinkling stars. When the train stopped, the ghost stepped off the track and disappeared into the rocks nearby."*

Is this the ghost of the fallen brakeman, the brave volunteer, the murdered conductor, or someone we totally don't know just yet, like Mr. Lawhead?

Now according to the Athens Messenger there are two known Lawheads that worked on the RR in this area. They are Theodore B. Lawhead (1844-?) showing to be alive at the time of the 1880 census and Theodore Alba Lawhead who was born Nov. 14th, 1878 and died on Jan. 27th, 1925. He had married Eedythe Alma Fuller (Nov. 18th, 1879-Oct., 1959) on October 2nd, 1901. Plus he had a sister who was married to Elmer Dixon of Mineral and another sister named Kate Lawhead.

The Engineer Lawhead, mentioned in the article, is obviously not the second Lawhead mentioned, but quite possibly the first one. So it is quite possible that at some time between 1880 and 1895 Theodore B. Lawhead 'lost his life' out on the Moonville/Mineral line somewhere.

Or maybe, this is the smallpox volunteer, that man I presume to be Dr. George Delos Coe, who had died trying to stop a train and save his town. Maybe he died on Feb. 11th, 1894 and his ghost came back on that anniversary.

Back in July of 1977, around 11:30 P.M, a fast-moving B&O freight train was heading west through the Moonville area. At the throttle was a 21 year old rookie engineer who was making only his third run on this line. Up to now, the run had been routine. However, all this changes as soon as they approach the Moonville Tunnel. About 500 yards ahead the rookie engineer sees a figure of a 'dark man' with a swinging lantern standing on the tracks before him. The 'dark man' is clearly seen swinging his lantern back and forth trying to get the train to stop. Is this the ghost of the fallen brakeman, the brave volunteer, the murdered conductor, Engineer Lawhead, or someone we totally don't know just yet?

As the rookie engineer prepares to put the train into emergency (bring the train to a quick and sudden stop), he is stopped by the more experienced conductor in charge. This particular conductor has seen this figure many times before. He tells the young engineer that in about 15 seconds he will understand why he should just keep on going. As the train approached the tunnel, running at about 50 mph, the lights from the engine could now make out the full figure of the man—but something was amiss. The light from the engine appeared to be going right through the man.

In just an instance the train was on top of the man, and then, the man was gone. Right before their very eyes the man vanishes. There was no scream that night as there had been in the past. Sometimes there are screams and other times there are not. The train just kept rolling right on over where the figure had stood and continued onward. The rookie engineer was quite visibly distraught over this and later on asked his supervisor for a new train route. Typically this incident happens over and over again until the trains stopped coming and the tracks were removed. The ghost seems to know that trains are no longer coming through the tunnel anymore. The Moonville ghost, or ghosts, has taken their toll on the trains.

Back in the summer of 1979 someone said they had seen one of the Moonville ghosts. The person relaying this next version was the driver of the car. It happened at the Moonville Tunnel.

Around 10 PM that summer evening six teenagers, of various ages, were walking back to their car from a nearby swimming hole along Raccoon Creek. (There's a good size swimming hole at the foot of the trestle columns, in Raccoon Creek, that lead back to the tunnel.) One of the older teens had bought some beer that night and shared a few with the teens that were underage. But only four may have been drinking. The driver indicated he had not been drinking since he was the driver.

As the six teens got closer to the tunnel, (now I like to know how they were heading to their car as they got closer to the tunnel when the road is in the opposite direction of the tunnel?) one of them spotted someone with a light following not to far behind them. Their concern was that this was a local sheriff, carrying a flashlight, trying to catch up to them. The teens had been making a lot of noise that night so they figured that someone from one of the nearby houses had called the local police on them. Therefore, two of the teens talked it over and decided to walk back to meet and talk with the sheriff while the rest continued to the car with the beer. These two teens thought it best to clear up everything with the officer and meet the others back at the car.

As they got about halfway through the tunnel, the one friend was closer to the light and the other a few steps behind. This friend saw his other friend go running past him in fright. His commotion caused everyone to take off running to the car. When they all got to the car these friends told the others that there was no one carrying that light.

So another friend, and the driver of the car himself, decided they would go and head back to the tunnel to see what it was that their friends had seen. Being the driver and he had not been drinking (supposedly) and his friend, who was walking with him, hadn't had any either (supposedly) believed they could make a fairer and more sober evaluation of what was supposedly seen.

As they got closer, the driver said it looked like someone was walking down the tracks with a lit lantern. However, as they got closer, they noticed that the light was glowing, but not casting any real light. Once they got within twenty yards of the light, they could make out a partial outline of the lantern. It was also clear to them *that no one was holding this lit lantern.* It was at this point the lantern stopped moving forward and then started to just swing back and forth.

Both young men turned around and bolted out of there as fast as they could, heading back to their car and their waiting friends. As the driver was leaving the area with his five friends in tow he could see the light and his response was *"Yes, it was in the tunnel just swinging away."*

So who was this ghost? Was it the fallen brakeman, the brave volunteer, the headless conductor, Engineer Lawhead, or is it the man in our next story that everyone thinks it is?

The Tall 'Dark' One

Within a few years after Moonville's establishment a family by the name of Dexter had moved there from the Commonwealth of Virginia. Their patriarch was Thomas Dexter (b. 1820 in Virginia—d.? Ohio) who was a freed slave who, along with his white wife, Margret (b. 1842 in Virginia—d.? Ohio; maiden name unknown and the daughter of a plantation owner) left Virginia to come to Ohio to make a new home for themselves.

Before arriving to Ohio they had wed in Virginia, in 1860, and had their first child, a son, named Albert that same year as well; which leads me to believe that they were romantically involved long before they got married and quite possibly were with child when they got married. (There relationship had to be something in and of itself in the area they hail from, considering all things of that period.)

By 1864 the Dexter's had left Virginia and moved to rural Ohio, settling in Waterloo, Athens County, to become farmers. Mr. and Mrs. Dexter eventually had eight more children that grew up in the Athens area; each being listed as a 'Mulatto' child in the 1880 Census. After Albert was Gaston (1864-?), then Erastus (1866-1920's), then Jasper (1868-?), then Formadell (1871-?) and Foedell (1871-?). Next was Castor (1873-?), then Bertha (1876-?), and finally Cashius (1879-?).

In total Mr. and Mrs. Dexter had nine children, 3 daughters—two being twins, and six boys. However, our interests lies with their third child, Erastus.

First, as you can see, Erastus Dexter was born in 1866 and never could have been the brakeman in the 1859 story.

Secondly, I have to speculate a little about the relationship between Thomas and Margret Dexter. Margret, having been the daughter of a plantation owner during the 1840's and 50's, would surely have received some kind of formal education and would have lived in a good God-fearing home with strong southern beliefs on slavery. So why in the world would she fell in love with a slave who was 22 years her senior, and marry him during such turbulent time as 1860? Being pregnant by him is one thing however, I have to speculate that she grew up watching him work around the plantation and became quite enamored of him; plus, she must grown into a free-thinking spirited young woman in her own right as well. Therefore, I must believe that Thomas had a good disposition about his place in life, at the time, which she thought was quite charming; however, I further speculate, that Margret didn't approve of the brutality of slavery that was quite common in America at that time and had let it known in her family circle, thereby causing her and her family considerable grief. (Plus, she would have had to become a slave herself since that was the custom, at that time, for having married a slave, moving from the main house to slave quarters and doing slave chores.)

Therefore, this must have put Margret and Thomas in a difficult position causing her to leave her family, the plantation, her comfortable surroundings, and her beloved Virginia to seek out a new place to live, a place that they could call their own.

And, I must say, that it must have been some kind of special love they had for each other in order to get married, (and to be allowed to) with her father's approval (or not), during such a time of deep racial segregation; unless of course, it was a "shotgun" wedding, which it may have been.

Either way, and there is no denying it, they loved each other very much regardless of the social values of that period and were willing to do what they had to do in order to be together in peace.

Now back to our main person of interest.

Erastus Dexter, and his siblings, would have grown up as free black children (which I'm sure is what Margret wanted), by loving, hardworking parents. The children would have attended local Moonville schools as much as any farmer's children could while also receiving lessons at home from their parents, which would include, I presume, that race should not be an issue in one's life as they grew to learn about the racial prejudices in the latter years of the 19th Century.

Therefore, I imagine, that the Dexter children would have cultivated a lot of friends of both races but, unfortunately, due to social morals and values in the late 19th and early 20th Centuries of southeastern Ohio many more would have been black than white.

Not much is known about Erastus' life, except to say, that by the time Erastus was a man he had come to work as a Moonville miner, like some of his other brothers, with his tale taking place in the 1920's when he would have been at least 54 years old, if not older, depending on what year this tale, his tale, actually took place. Whether he was married and had children is not known, but I would presume so. Why he may have been, quite possibly, a grandparent himself who to this day may have descendants still living in the region.

    The Moonville tale about a supposed eight foot tall black man, with a white beard, who walks like he is on stilts, wearing a miner's hat with an oil lamp on his head, wearing dirty overalls from working that day, and carrying a lantern who was killed in either 1920, or the 1920's, by an oncoming train through the Moonville tunnel was, in my opinion, Erastus Dexter.

    After a hard day's work Erastus, and a group of other black miners and a few railroad workers, decided to play some poker and drink some moonshine or whiskey, in a shanty-shack that was nearby the tracks. (One account said they were in the saloon. If that were true these men would have been in Moonville, playing poker, which is west of the tunnel and across the Raccoon Creek train-trestle.) So off they went to this nearby shack and commenced to play poker that evening while drinking a lot of moonshine, just whiling away the night talking about mining, railroading and of course women, amongst other things. Why I imagine they may even had some cigars, a banjo and did some singing too. I have the feeling that this must have been a Friday or a Saturday night after a good week of working. (However, the time of year is not known.)

    Before long the men were drunk, feeling good but knew they had to call it a night since it was getting very late, or very early in the morning, (depending on how you want to look at it). Therefore, they broke up their game and were soon on their way, heading to their respective homes.

    Erastus Dexter, I'm sure, was feeling quite drunk as he was heading to his home, which he had to get to by going through the Moonville Tunnel. With the town being west of the tunnel he would have had to walk across the trestle over Raccoon Creek and make his way to the tunnel, if they were playing in town. But if the shack was on the east side of the tunnel then he had to head west through the tunnel; and I can just imagine that he was singing and a whistlin' a miner's song as he went.

    However, he wasn't paying too much attention to things going on around him, as is common with inebriated folks while making his way through the tunnel, when he heard a sound coming up from behind him as he shuffled along the tracks. When he turned around he saw a train heading straight towards him. He obviously wasn't as alert and clear thinking as he should have been and got off the tracks and out of the tunnel. What he did was try and slow the train down to a stop by waving his lantern, and arms, back and forth in an attempt to stop the train. Unfortunately his efforts proved to be quite futile because the conductors and engineer didn't see him soon enough due to the billowing smoke and steam thereby not having enough time to stop the train. Erastus was struck by the train and slammed into the brick wall of the tunnel, being instantly killed. This was most certainly a tragic and unfortunate accident for the community of Moonville.

Reportedly, Erastus Dexter is buried in the Moonville graveyard.

Erastus' ghost, like the other two mentioned before, is described as being an eight foot tall 'dark' man, with a whitish gray beard, who walks like he is on stilts while wearing a miner's cap with an oil lamp on his head and a lantern in his left-hand (I presume) while dressed in dirty overalls. His eyes are supposedly like glistening balls of fire with flame flowing backwards over his shoulders for hair as he walks down the tracks, which are now no longer there.

Sometimes, it is said, that he appears quite often while other times it may be years before he is sited again.

Now just switch Erastus with the brakeman, the conductor, the brave volunteer, or Engineer Lawhead and you got the same ghost, but with a different occupation.

It has also been mentioned that another Dexter lost his life to the tracks as well. Presumably it was a brother, but which one is not known. Either Jasper or Gaston, I suppose.

Therefore, if anytime you see a large 'dark' male wondering the woods of Moonville, say hello, for it is more and likely Erastus Dexter.

The Haunting Ladies

There is a tale of a woman that died out in Moonville, along the tracks, that use to wear lavender perfume. It said that her scent can be smelled just off of where the train-trestle use to be.

Between Moonville, to the west, and the tunnel, to the east, lies Raccoon Creek where M&C RR built a bridge using five separate concrete support columns in order to allow trains to cross. The columns are said to be 50 ft. high (30 feet must be buried underground because only 20 feet or so is exposed from the ground up) and built only wide enough for the track to be laid across them.

However, many deaths have occurred from where this train-trestle use to be as individuals tried to cross over it and were surprised by an oncoming speeding train. Anyone caught in the middle of the trestle had but two choices: either face certain death by train or face a most certain bone breaking leap into the shallow rock-strewn creek below. Therefore, any unlucky soul who found themselves caught halfway across the trestle by an oncoming train usually just froze with horrified fright and died instantly after being slammed into by the oncoming train.

And, apparently, it appears, it was the women who were usually caught out on the train-trestles.

According to the Athens Messenger there was a woman (old or young is not known, nor neither is her name) who was killed instantly on the morning of October 12th, 1873 (a Sunday) while walking from the town of Mineral to Moonville. She was attempting to cross the Raccoon Creek train-trestle in front of the tunnel when she was struck and instantly killed by an oncoming morning express. She was found lying in the creek-bed below.

45

Whether she died from being hit by the train or from the fall is not known. However, it is said that one can get a whiff of stale lavender once, whoever, gets to the other side (presumably the side with the tunnel) and takes a short trail off of the old gravel path. Is this the lady that is known as the "Lavender Lady of Moonville"?

Or is this lady our 'Lavender Lady'? There is a tale of a young headless female ghost that has been seen walking eastward towards Ingham Station from Moonville Tunnel. Apparently, the young woman was walking from Moonville to Ingham Station, just a mile east of Moonville, deciding to take a short cut through the tunnel rather than climb over the steep hillside, which makes sense. But, unfortunately, once inside the tunnel, she was caught by an oncoming westbound train and with no place to run to she was ran over and decapitated.

It has been said that this ghost of this young woman will quicken her pace if anyone should approach her. And if they get to close she will dart into the tunnel and disappear.

I wonder why?

And as to when this happened, it is not known.

In 1886, it is said, that a young mature woman wearing a blue night-gown, who was possibly pregnant, was either just wandering around the tracks about a mile from the Moonville tunnel on a train-trestle (east or west of it is not known but east is presumed) or she was on her way to see a lover when she was caught unaware on the trestle by an oncoming train. She began waving her lantern and arms in order to stop the train but was unable to avoid it, and was thus decapitated and killed.

Today, if you see a blue orb, it is presumed to be this woman. Also she has been known to wonder around the area in her blue night gown at night. Her ghost is said to roam the old train-trestle, looking for her lost head.

With the train trestles now gone, I wonder where she roams?

This next tale, and quite possibly a fictitious tale at that, is of a woman who had very recently given birth and did not want to keep her new born. (It is not known whether this incident happened in the late 19th or early 20th century, or if she happened to live in Moonville or drove out there from somewhere else.) Therefore, she took her newborn down to the one lane bridge that extends Shea Road over Raccoon Creek and carried the unsuspecting child under the bridge. Once there she submerged her newborn into the icy cold water, holding it down until it drowned.

What the woman did after that is not known. Did she leave the baby there or did she take the baby back home and perform a burial of some kind? Did she do something to herself afterwards for what she did; or did someone else realize what she had done and had her taken care of?

And what of the baby's father? Did he know? Did he care? Or was he the reason why she did this such horrendous deed to her own flesh and blood?

Now, supposedly, at midnight on a night during a phase called a 'waxing moon', which comes after a new moon where the lighted portion of the moon is gradually increasing from a thin crescent on the right-hand side, when you stop your car in the middle of the one-lane bridge, and turn it off, placing your keys on the hood (what the purpose behind this is and why this should matter to a ghost is not known), or if you just park your car, get out and go and stand in the middle of the bridge and remain absolutely quiet you are supposedly able to hear the sound of a crying baby.

So, it is said.

This next accident occurred sometime around 1905. There was a youthful looking middle-aged woman, who appears to be in her 40's, (meaning she was born just sometime after the end of the Civil War) wearing a white turn of the century (19th to the 20th) outfit, carrying a lantern. She is supposedly seen walking along the side the railroad tracks (when they use to be there) heading towards the tunnel.

Apparently this lady was walking home to Moonville from the town of Mineral, which, as has been mentioned before, is to the east and a few miles away. (It would be a good two to three hour walk.) When she was only about one mile from the Moonville tunnel, crossing a train-trestle, she was struck by an oncoming train and killed.

Today people see a female ghost walking along the tracks just outside of the tunnel, carrying a lantern and dressed in a flowing white dress or robe. From her appearance, she is clearly not solid, nor does she give off any light, however, those that say they have seen her, have said, they couldn't see anything on the other side of her.

This ghost, it has been said, appears to hikers and apparently, at one time, someone had seen her and called out to her. This apparition of this lady turned and looked at them—just for a brief moment—while continuing to walk away; and within a few moments the lady disappeared around the bend, presumably still heading for home.

It is said that her ghost can be seen near the tunnel, at night, still wearing her white gown.

Our next tale is about a lady named Mrs. Patrick Shea. Mrs. Shea was an elderly lady in her eighties and was the grandmother to Michael Shea. With Mike being born in 1891, I will presume that Mrs. Shea's incident happened sometime considerably after his birth in the early to the mid years of the 20th century.

Mrs. Shea, who was a Moonville resident wanted, or needed, to go to Hope one day. She set out walking to Hope and was, unfortunately, caught out on the Raccoon Creek train-trestle. Once she got out onto the trestle she was struck by a train that came through the Moonville Tunnel, heading west bound. Mrs. Shea, due to her advanced age, was just simply too old to run fast enough and too scared to jump off the trestle and hence she was hit by the fast oncoming train. Mrs. Shea had lost a leg to amputation and later died from shock.

Back in the 1970's a group of girls were hiking the tracks when they spotted a young girl, or young woman, sitting at the far end of the tunnel; however, she disappeared when they attempted to approach her.

This young female, supposedly, was walking along the train-trestle when a fast-moving train came upon her causing her to fall to her death into Raccoon Creek.

Other hikers have also complained of the girl, or woman, following them along on the trail.

And since this happened before our next tale, I have to presume, it is yet another little girl or young woman.

In 1986, the last person known to be killed by an oncoming train near the Moonville Tunnel was that of a ten year old girl. (Who she was is not known, nor the time of year.) She was killed by an oncoming CSX train about two months after CSX had, *supposedly*, abandoned using the line. (CSX reportedly stopped using the line on August 31st, 1985, meaning that this little girl may have been killed as early as late October of 1985; and word of her demise, at this location, did not begin to spread until 1986.)

She was supposedly playing on, or near, the train-trestle that leads back to the tunnel when the CSX train struck and killed her. It is said that people can still hear a little girl's haunting laugh when they get near the tunnel entrance.

So please be sure to stop and say hello to her when you get ready to enter the tunnel.

Back in 1998 there was a 105 year old woman who had lived in Moonville as a child and as an adult. By 1998 she lived seven miles south of Moonville and no longer discussed anything about her life there.

I wonder why?

Murdered Men

There was a man who was murdered late one night as he walked home along the tracks. It began when he got into a barroom brawl at a local saloon with a couple of other men. It was either quite possibly the fight was over a poker game where someone might have been cheating or over money owed; or maybe even over a woman.

Eyewitnesses say that the man was very drunk and had trouble walking steadily. He had staggered out of the saloon as he headed back towards Moonville. (I thought the saloon was in Moonville which gives credence to a possible second saloon in the area. Or, just maybe, he was in a nearby shanty shack that was a make-shift saloon that served moonshine.) However, it is believed that the men with whom he was fighting had left the saloon before he did and hid out in the nearby woods; and as the man staggered by they bushwhacked him along side the tracks, quite possibly robbing him before they murdered him, leaving his dead body on the tracks.

Despite the fact that the dead body had been run over by a, or several, trains the coroner confirmed and stated that the man was dead before a train had hit him.

Unfortunately, his murderers were never found.

Having a lantern was never mentioned either, nor was there ever a date given as to when this happened.

In 1936 a man was murdered at the Moonville Inn. How and why he was murdered is not known, but robbery is suspected. Many people do claim to see this ghost, of the murdered man, standing near the top of the tunnel, to the right, where the inn was said to be. (Facing east, into the tunnel, with back towards the trestle columns and the road beyond.)

A Suicide

According to a great-granddaughter, a young lady named Erin, her great-grandfather Amzey or Amza (some accounts say his name is Amos) Kennard, was accidentally killed when he stepped in front of a fast oncoming train. However, Erin states that Amzey, sometime in the 1920's, was involved in a mining accident that required him to have surgery and get a metal plate inserted into his skull.

The mining incident that killed Raymond Burritt in 1919 was the last one listed as ever happening and it caused the mining operations in Moonville to be closed. Could Amzey have been hurt by this same incident? Unfortunately that is not known. After that incident Amzey was considered by the locals to be what was then known as *'touched in the head'*, but a good fella.

Sometime in the 1930's Amzey was diagnosed with prostate cancer and was in considerable pain. Having been a conductor when he was a young man Amzey knew when the trains ran through Moonville. So on one particular Mother's Day he went around the household saying good-bye to his relatives, but they all thought he was just being Amzey—'touched in the head'.

After completing his rounds in the house Amzey went out into the garden to ask his son Donald what time it was. Donald told him and Amzey thanked him. Amzey, recalling the train schedules, walked to the nearby tracks at the appropriate time and stepped in front of an oncoming train.

The engineer, upon seeing the man on the track, tried to stop the train, slamming on the brakes. The engineer caused such a commotion with sounding of the horn and the screeching of the brakes that it notified the Kennard family of what Amzey Kennard had just done.

It was left to Donald to pick up his father's various remains from the tracks.

A Bizarre Accident

In 1954 Charles Ferguson (1927?-1954) was a young man in his late 20s. He, however, was run over in a very peculiar and odd way. His death is one of the more bizarre tales coming out of Moonville concerning a freak accident that took place between the tunnel and the train-trestle, costing him his young life.

On his way to somewhere Charles Ferguson walked up to the edge of the tracks and saw an oncoming train coming and knew he had to patiently wait for it to pass before crossing over the tracks. Once the train went by Charles stepped up and started to cross the tracks since the train he had waited on to pass had done so.

Apparently, somewhere along the track, the back part of the train had become uncoupled from the front part and was now in two distinct sections. Without knowing this Charles, stepped out onto the track after the first section went by, thinking the whole train had just passed and without, apparently, bothering to look both ways, stepped out in front of the second section still coming through.

Mr. Ferguson's accident was certainly most unfortunate.

Today many people claim to see a red, glowing form (why red and glowing is not known) near the tunnel, who they believe to be Charles Ferguson.

David's Story

The Sunday, October 31st, 1993 Athens Messenger tells a story of a student by the name of David from Ohio University, who, along with three friends went to the Moonville Tunnel area to have a swim in the Raccoon Creek.

There are two sizable swimming holes in the area; and ghosts, or spirits, are said to be, supposedly, attracted to bodies of water. One swimming hole is near the tunnel at the bottom of trestle columns; and the other one is located back across the road, heading further west at the bottom of another set of trestle columns.

Each are connected with Raccoon Creek.

Sometime before, or after, swimming they decided to go and have a look at the tunnel. On their way back through the tunnel, about halfway in, they saw a light. (Didn't say which side of the tunnel, but it is presumed the west-end.) They decided to split into two groups since they had beer, because two of the four were underage, with those two, the minors, going on to the car while the other two headed to investigate the light.

These two young men proceeded towards the light and in a matter of a few minutes were soon running out of the tunnel, shouting *"There is no one carrying the light!"* David, being a bit skeptic at what his friends were saying, decided to go back into the tunnel and to have another look for himself. Then, within a few minutes, David comes running out, shouting, *"He wasn't kidding!"*

Later on, David also said, *"It was just a swinging light with no one holding it. I high-tailed it back to the car. I haven't been out there since."*

Apparently there was a spirit swinging a lantern, not showing itself, looking for a train; or its head.

The Ohio Exploration Society

The following is a paraphrased narrative from the Ohio Exploration Society (OES) website concerning Moonville Tunnel. The OES investigates and reports on paranormal activity and were last known to be lead by Jason Robinson. He's other investigators include Jason Colwell, Misty Jones and Abraham Bartlett, and they are all from Columbus, Ohio. From what I have read on OES they seem to be quite sincere and thorough in their research of paranormal activity.

OES visited Moonville Tunnel on Saturday, April 6th, 2002, and according to the OES, they got very high EMF (electromagnetic frequency or static) readings within Moonville Tunnel indicating a high probability of ghostly or paranormal activity. However, their first attempt for an EVP (electronic voice phenomena) failed when the tape they were using snapped in half right near the middle of the tunnel. If there was something there, it sure didn't want them to hear it.

(There seems to be several such incidences occurring in the middle of that tunnel. There are several accounts online where people tell of such events happening, such as cameras or flashlights malfunctioning.)

In June of 2003, the OES returned to Moonville hoping to finally get some EVP. They apparently were not disappointed. Not only did they get a few strange occurrences on tape, one of the members actually saw the ghostly lantern himself while others witnessed a dark shadowy figure at the western end of the tunnel. They also said they experienced lighting changes in the tunnel where the tunnel became slightly darker for brief moments of time. Their female member (I presume Ms. Jones) experienced extreme cold-chills and the pictures taken near her showed a blue orb. (Is this our pregnant woman's ghost?) While she was taking an EVP, a voice said *"I got you."*

Again the OES returned to Moonville Tunnel with a documentary team on Tuesday, October 19th, 2004. They arrived at the tunnel around 6:30 P.M. and began their investigation. According to the OES the tunnel was unusually dark when they stood in the center and a fog rolled in. After walking the entire length of the tunnel and not picking up any out-of-the-ordinary readings on the EMF Meter, they decided to stand in the center of the tunnel with their lights out. After a few minutes, while staying quiet and trying to capture an EVP they heard a sound coming from the Raccoon Creek, or western, end of the tunnel, but it was most likely water dripping from the ceiling. As everyone looked in that direction, the OES Founder, Jason Robinson, decided to look at the other end of the tunnel where he witnessed a dim light. He informed the group of eight people about the light, but as with many things paranormal, the light disappeared as soon as they turned to look.

(What is it, or why is it, that we, mortals, are not suppose to see them? What is it about the nature of God's world that refuses us to see disembodied spirits?)

As the group stood looking toward where the light had been seen, the eastern end of the tunnel, there was a sudden scuffling sound of someone, or something, coming down the hill, just outside of the tunnel. The footsteps were very distinctive and were in the middle of the gravel path and started to sprint directly towards the entire group. At first, they thought, that someone might be playing a trick on them. Therefore, two members turned their flashlights on and pointed them in the direction of the sound of that someone running. The sound immediately stopped and nothing was seen. Jason Robinson and the head of the documentary team walked to the end of the tunnel, not seeing the source of the running.

However, they had other signs of paranormal activity taking place. When two members reached the end of the tunnel, the temperature dropped a measurable 10-15°F to 40°F and the EMF reading was at the top of the scale and not budging. Furthermore, there was a very thick static electricity feeling in the air and the fog was so thick that no one could see 10ft in front of themselves. As the rest of the group arrived at the tunnel's end, a very strong smell of musk cologne overwhelmed everyone. The thick fog, the coldness, and the smell dissipated after about one minute.

An EVP was captured by the documentary crew, the voice stating, *"Come closer"*, just before the running was heard. It was truly one of the most intense moments the OES has experienced while conducting an investigation.

A Boy Saved by a Ghost

There is one instance where a young boy was saved by a ghost. As the young lad approached the tunnel from the west end, the ghost suddenly appeared and screamed at the boy—*"Get out!"*. The boy became so frighten that he turned around and ran the other way. He had ran no more than a few feet when he looked back, looking for the ghost which was no longer there—only seeing the oncoming lights of a speeding train coming into the tunnel from the other side. If he had kept on walking he would have been in the tunnel as the train was coming through, killing him instantly, for sure.

Fortunately, for the young lad (now presumably a grown man) had stepped off the track just in time; and to this day he, presumably, has never gone back out to Moonville as far as anyone knows. As to when this happened was not documented.

Finally, a young boy apparently broke his thumb while playing with a grave marker one day up at the Moonville graveyard. Somehow it toppled over, landed on his hand and broke his thumb. This was, most likely, an unfortunate accident and not caused by any malcontent spirits; but, then again, one should not go around playing in graveyards; just in case.

When this happened is not known.

Parting Thoughts

As you can tell Moonville is a rather unique place with many intriguing stories and anyone who has been out there will tell you that Moonville is a fascinating place to see. And as a place of historical fascination I say that Moonville Tunnel is truly deserving of preservation not only as a memorial to Ohio history, but to the pioneering spirit of the Coe family as well as to the many other hard-working individuals who lived and died out there.

Therefore, it is my hope that the State of Ohio will find in its heart, and budget, to preserve this tunnel, and its surrounding grounds, thus allowing for a bike trail to go through this area that would be managed by the good folks of MRTA.

It would certainly have my vote.

Now on to the most pressing question of this book—who is the true Moonville Ghost? There have been so many unfortunate deaths in and around Moonville it would be impossible to say who is exactly the true Moonville ghost; however, I personally think it is the brave smallpox volunteer—Dr. George Delos Coe; and I believe he died on or about February the 11th of 1894, going for help.

And as for the tall 'dark' one, that is most certainly Erastus Dexter.

And as for the one holding the lantern, waving it in the tunnel, that may very well be the murdered Conductor. And I'd be careful of him, he has a score to settle.

Each ghost is, or was, known to warn the living about being in that tunnel when a train was coming; but now that the trains no longer come through there what have they to do but wait for you to come and visit them.

I hope you have found this history of Moonville and its haunting legends enlightening; and if you get a chance to visit Moonville please don't forget to say hello to all the ghosts out there, for you never know who is listening—or watching you. And if you happen to see a ghost, or a lantern waving in the wind, don't be frighten and run away—or run towards them—for they are just as curious about you as we are of them. Just wave, take your pictures, and move on.

WILLIAM M. CULLEN

And one last note, if you should have enjoyed this work and wish to share your thoughts or comments with me, or if you happen to know anything else of these events, or who some of these people were, or have any new information, please email me at cullen_w@msn.com. I would certainly appreciate the information.

Thank you.

Directions to Moonville Tunnel

First find and locate Lake Hope State Park on any Ohio map or *Mapquest*. Lake Hope State Park is located in Vinton County, which is next to Athens County in southeastern Ohio. Also, the town of McArthur is the County Seat of Vinton County.

Once at Lake Hope State Park (which has facilities by the way) you'll need to locate Wheelabout Road. If you come down from the north by way of Nelsonville it will be on your left-hand side, just north of Lake Hope State Park. If you come up by way of McArthur and Zaleski it will be on your right-hand side, just a little north of Lake Hope State Park. This will be Wheelabout Road—a.k.a. Township Highway 18. Turn down here and drive slowly because in just a few short seconds, about 2/10 of a mile, you will come to a fork in the road—I suggest you take it.

You'll take the gravel road to your left, avoiding the sharp curve to your right. You're now on Hope-Moonville Road. (It also has been referred to as Shea Road but Shea Road is actually only a small part of the whole road; plus local county maps call it Hope-Moonville Road.)

Follow this narrow gravel road carefully. After a few minutes (2-3) you'll come up a hill that leads to a very sharp—and I mean very sharp—hair-pin curve; slowly—and I mean slowly—follow through it. (Don't worry about the side road you see, it just a short cut-through road that goes to the other side.) Then keep on going down the other side and after a few minutes more (another 2-3) you'll come to a steel-truss one-lane bridge crossing Raccoon Creek.

Immediately following this bridge, about 100 feet or so, (so go slowly) you'll see the old the gravel roadbed where railroad tracks used to cross the road. The roadbed is distinguishable as a straight gravel roadbed that crosses the road and goes in both directions. You need to park where you can. Be mindful of wet and muddy ground. You do not want to get stuck out there, for there is no wireless phone service. (Plus there are no facilities. It is a very rural and remote area. So plan accordingly.)

Walk down the roadbed path to the left. After a short walk you will come to the concrete trestle columns. Back over to your right you'll see a path that goes down to Raccoon Creek. At the bottom of the path you can cross the creek on a rock path and then climb up the other side; providing, of course, that it is not flooded over. Once you get the up the other embankment you'll see the tunnel.

Now if Raccoon Creek is flooded then all you need to do is walk back down Hope-Moonville Road from which you came, crossing the bridge, and there you'll find another path. Many people use this route anyway, it's only a little longer.

To see the house foundations, climb up the embankment on the right-side of the tunnel entrance. There's a visible flat place in an otherwise sloping area. This was where the inn used to be.

To see the cemetery, which I recommend first, continue on down Hope-Moonville Road about a ¼ mile, away from the bridge, and you'll soon see a side service-road up to your right. It curves up and around, ending at the cemetery. It is said that here you might see a ghost or two there, one being that Union soldier.

And finally, please be respectful of the whole area for it is State and privately owned property and rangers, as well as county police, do patrol the area.

Thank you.

Bibliography

Books, Newspapers & Magazines:

Athens Messenger, The; Thursday, October 16th, 1873.

Athens Messenger, The; Thursday, Jan., 7th, 1886, "The County Mirrored".

Athens Messenger, The; Thursday, May 20th, 1886, "The County Mirrored", p. 1; col. 6.

Athens Messenger & Herald, The; Thursday, March 31st, 1892, "The County Mirrored", p5, col. 2.

Athens Messenger & Herald, The; Thursday, August 11, 1892, "The County Mirrored", P5, col. 2,

Athens Messenger & Herald, The; Thursday, March 22nd, 1894, "The County Mirrored", p. 1, col. 2,

Athens Messenger & Herald, The; Thursday, April 19, 1894, "The County Mirrored", p.1, col. 3,

Athens Messenger & Herald, The; Thursday, July 5th, 1894, "The County Mirrored", p. 1, col. 1,

Athens Messenger & Herald, The; Thursday, July 26, 1894, *"Stamping out a pest—How Milwaukee's Health Dept. Treats Smallpox"*, P6, Col. 1,

Athens Messenger & Herald, The; Thursday, August 16th, 1894. "The County Mirrored" P.1, Col. 1.

Athens Messenger & Herald, The; Thursday, August 23rd, 1894, "The County Mirrored",

Athens Messenger & Herald, The; Thursday, September 27, 1894, "The County Mirrored", P 1. Col 3

Athens Messenger & Herald, The; 1894; *"Smallpox Patients: How they are handled in the big city of Chicago"*, p.2, col. 4

Athens Messenger, The; Monday, October 10th, 1932, P. 5, col. 5. *"Railroads of this district in early days are recalled"*

Athens Messenger, The; Thursday, May 8th, 1975

Athens Messenger, The; Sunday, June 30th, 1991

Athens Messenger, The; Sunday; April 25th, 1999.

Blum, Deborah, *"Ghost Hunters: William James and the Search for Scientific Proof of Life After Death."* The Penguin Press, NY, 2006.

Botkin, B. A.; *"A Treasury of American Folklore: Stories, Ballads, and Traditions of the People"*; Crown Publishers; N.Y.; 1944.

Chillicothe *Gazette,* The; Sunday, February 17th, 1895.

Claussen, Nick; The Athens News, Thursday, April 15th, 2004. *"Rail trail may go as far as Moonville"*

Columbus, Dispatch, The; *"The Ghost of Moonville and Other Ohio Spooks"*, Sunday, October 25th, 1981.

Cross, Roy. *"Apparitions Still at Home in the Hills of Vinton County: No Better time for a Ghost-chasing Trek or Tale"*, Athens Messenger, The; Sunday, October 31st, 1993.

Dilts, James D.; *The Great Road: The Building of the Baltimore & Ohio, The Nation's First Rail Road, 1828-1853.*; Stanford University Press, Stanford California; 1993; P. XIX under Chronology.

Everett, Lawrence, *"Ghosts and Legends of Southeastern Ohio and Beyond: Tales of Legends, Hauntings and the Unexplained"*, Infinity Publishing, Haverford, Pa., October 2003. P. 31.

"Ghosts of Moonville Tale Stirs Memories", Columbus Citizen's Journal, The; Friday, April 3rd, 1970

"Ghosts in Ohio State Parks." Wednesday, October 27th, 1982.

"History of Hocking County—1883", Reproduction by Anagraphic, Inc. 1974, Chicago Inter-State Publishing Co., 1883. P.799.

Haining, Peter; *"The Clans of Darkness: Scottish Stories of Fantasy & Horror"*; Taplinger Publishing Co.; N.Y.; 1971.

Jordan, Phillip D. *The History of the State of Ohio: Ohio Comes of Age 1873-1900. Vol. V."* Ohio State Archaeological and Historical Society, Columbus, Ohio, 1943. Reprinted 1968.

Kachuba, John, *"Ghost Hunters: On the Trail of Mediums, Dowsers, Spirit Seekers, and Other Investigators of America's Paranormal World"*, Career Press, Inc.; Franklin Lakes, NJ; 2007. P. 139-146.

Kuhn, Megan; Action; Thursday, Feb, 7th, 2002; *"From railroad town to ghost town in 100 years"*

McArthur Democrat, The; Tuesday, March 29th 1859

McCready, Albert L.; *Railroads in the Days of Steam*; American Heritage Publishing C., Inc., N.Y. 1960. P. 100-101

Mitro, Angela, Athens Messenger, The; *"Plans for Moonville Rail Trail are Rolling Ahead."*, Wednesday, April 14th, 2004.

Parsley, Betty Jo, The Athens Messenger. No date given for article.

Price, Bill., *"Up on the Ridge: Moonville is Now Deserted."* Athens Messenger, The; Sunday, March 28th, 1971.

Reamer, Charles W., The Athens Messenger: No date given for article.

Republican Tribune, The; *"75 Years Ago—1895. Who Remembers the Ghost of Moonville?"* Thursday, February 19th, 1970.

Scioto Gazette, The; Wednesday, January 2nd, 1895

Stover, John F.; History of the Baltimore & Ohio Rail Road; Purdue University Press; West Lafayette, Indiana; 1987. P. 82, 84-6, 88, & 97.

Thay, Edrick, *Ghost Stories of Ohio*, "The Moonville Ghost", Ghost House Books, 2001, P.148-152.

Tingley, Steve, *"People Pack Park Lodge to Plan and Discuss Moonville Trail."*, Athens Messenger, The; Sunday, November 24th, 2002.

Tingley, Steve, *"Support is Growing for Establishment of Moonville Trail"*, Vinton County Courier, The; Saturday, November 1st, 2003.

Tolliver, George, *"Letter to the Editor—Moonville Ghost."* Republican Tribune, The; Friday, March 26th, 1971.

"Vinton County Ohio: History and Families.", Turner Publishing, P.O. Box 3101, Paducah, Ky., 42002, P. 80, Col. 1 & 2.

Vinton County Courier, The; Wednesday, August 6th, 1975.

Vinton County Courier, The; Wednesday, October 1st, 1986.

Vinton County Courier, The; Wednesday, March 18th, 1998.—Editorial cartoon and article.

Vinton County Courier, The; *"Moonville Rail Trail, Inc. to Elect Board Members at April 28th Meeting"*, Wednesday, April 9th, 2003.

Webster's New World Dictionary of American English: Third College Edition, MacMillian Inc., USA.

Willis, James A., Henderson, Andrew, Coleman, Loren; *Weird Ohio*; Sterling Publishing Co., Inc.; NY; 2005. P. 25-29.

Woodyard, Chris; *"Haunted Ohio: Ghostly Tales from the Buckeye State"*; Krestel Publication; Beavercreek, Ohio; 1991. *"The Headless Conductor of Moonville"*; P92-93.

World Almanac and Book of Facts 2010, The; World Almanac Books; Nov. 2009, NY

Internet:

www.bioguide.congress.gov/scripts/biodisplay.pl
www.care2.com/c2c/groups/disc.html
www.catskillarchive.com/rrextra/glossry1.Html
www.centralohioparanormal.com/moonvilletunnel.htm
www.clevelandsupernatural.com/02-Moonville.html
www.en.wikipedia.org/wiki/Marietta_Subdivision.html
www.en.wikipedia.org/wiki?Moonville_Ohio.html
www.familysearch.orq
www.forgottenoh.com/moonville.html
www.ghoststudy.com/a_what_are_orbs.html
www.graveaddiction.com/moontun.html

WILLIAM M. CULLEN

www.hauntedhocking.com/Haunted_Ohio_Moonville_Tunnel.html
www.home.fuse.net/moonville.html
www.moonvillerailtrail.com
www.ohioexploration.com/moonvilletunnel.html
www.ohiotrespassers.com/moon.html
www.paranormalplus.com/new_page_6.htm
www.scripophily.net/marcinrailra.html
www.shadowseekers.org/moonville.html
www.spikesys.com/Trains/moonville.html
www.trainweb.org/utahrails/raillingo.html
www.users.3z.net/~jschmidt/moonvilleghost/index.shtml
www.waymarking.com/waymarks/WM247N
www.webmd.com
www.youtube.com/moonville

Index

A

Albany, Athens County, Ohio,
Ashtabula County,
Athens Masonic Temple,
Athens Messenger,
Athens (Ohio),
Athens County,
Athens County Historical Society,
Athens Masonic Temple,
Athens Messenger,
Athens Presbyterian Church,
Auditor of Athens County,

B

Baltimore & Ohio Railroad (B&O),
B&O Southwestern,
Balls of fire (eyes of),
Barbar or Barber, Mary Jane,
Bartlett, Abraham,
Belpre (Ohio),
Belpre and Cincinnati Railroad,
Biddle, Dr. Asher,
Biddle, Dr. David H.,
Big Run,
Bike trail,
Boxcars or freight cars,
Brakemen,
Brown Township,

Burritt, Raymond,
Byer, (Ohio),

C

Campbell, Laura P.,
Carbondale, (Ohio),
Cass, W.V.,
Chesapeake and Ohio Railway (C&O),
Chessie System Express (CSX),
Chicago,
Chillicothe (Ohio),
Chillicothe Gazette,
Cincinnati (Ohio),
Cincinnati Furnace,
Civil War,
Coe, Chester,
Coe, Cliff,
Coe, Frank R.,
Coe, George Albert,
Coe, George Delos (Dr.),
Coe, Josiah,
Coe, Lovisa,
Coe, Lucius Q. C.,
Coe, Martie,
Coe, Roxanna (Eggleston),
Coe, Samuel, (Mr.)
Coe, Wellington,
Columbus (Ohio),
Colwell, Jason,

Conductor(s),
Conductor (headless),
Connecticut,
Cox, William A.,
Cumberland,
Cutler, William Parker,
Currier sisters,

D

David's Story,
Dellinger, Thomas,
Dexter, Albert,
Dexter, Bertha,
Dexter, Cashius,
Dexter, Castor,
Dexter, Erastus, (Bub),
Dexter, Foedell,
Dexter, Formadell,
Dexter, Gaston,
Dexter, Jasper,
Dexter, Margret,
Dexter, Thomas,
Dixon, Elmer,
Dummery, Mr.,

E

Electromagnetic Frequency (EMF),
Erin (granddaughter to Amzy Kennard),
Electronic voice phenomena (EVP),

F

Fasley, Tom,
Ferguson, Charles,
Franklin and Ohio Railroad,
Forestry Division,
Fuller, Eedythe Alma,

G

Goldsberry, Frank,
Granville, Hampden County, Massachusetts,
'grip' the,
Grosvenor,

H

Hamden,
Haney, John,
Harmar,
Haunting Ladies,
Hemolytic Strepococci, hey days,
"Highways" (magazine),
Hocking Adena Bikeway,
Hocking River,
Hope (Ohio),
Hope School Interpretive Center,
Hope Furnace,
Hope Furnace Station,
Hope Hollow,
Hope-Moonville Road,

I

Ingham Station (Ohio),
Interstate Commerce Commission (ICC),

J

Jackson County (Ohio),
James, Clelie,
Jerseyville (now Shade),
Jesus,
Jones, Misty,

K

Kennard, Amzey,
Kennard, Charlotte,
Kennard, Donald,

Kennedy, Ada,
King's Tunnel,
King's Switch (Ohio),

L

Lake Hope State Park,
Lake Hope State Park Lodge,
Lavender (scent),
Lawhead, Kate,
Lawhead, Theodore Alba,
Lawhead, Engineer Theodore B.,
Lawhead, Mrs.,
Lincoln, Abraham,
Link-and-pin coupler,
Lookout Rock,

M

Mace Family,
Marietta College,
Marietta (Ohio),
Marietta & Cincinnati Railroad (M&C),
McArthur Democrat, The,
McArthur (Ohio),
McGill, Mary E.,
McKibben, Josephine,
Milwaukee,
Mining accident,
Mines,
Miners,
Mineral (Ohio),
Missouri,
Moon (man named),
Moonville (Ohio),
Moonville Cemetery,
Moonville Depot,
Moonville General store,
Moonville Inn,
Moonville Rail Trail Association (MRTA),
Moonville Station,
Moonville Tunnel,

Moore's Junction (Ohio),
Murdered men,

N

Nelsonville (Ohio),
Newcomb, Emeline,
Newcomb, Clara (Shint),
Newcomb, Thomas,
Northwestern Virginia RR,

O

Oak Grove Cemetery,
Ohio,
Ohio Exploration Society (OES),
Ohio & Mississippi RR,
Ohio River,
Ohio State House of Representatives,
Ohio University,
Ohio University—Alden Library,
O'Neal, Mattie,

P

Parkersburg, (W.) Va.,
Pinney, Teeney,
Plaque,
Pompey, Onondaga County, New York,
Pompey, New York,
Post office,

Q

Quarantine,
Queen City,

R

Raccoon Creek,
Raccoon Creek Valley,
Rannells (Dr.),

Rarely Herd,
Red Diamond,
Red and green lantern,
Roach, Harry,
Robinson, Jason,
Rome, Ashtabula County, Ohio,
Rue, Athens County, Ohio,
Rue, Moonville, Athens County, Ohio,
Rue Woods,

S

St. Louis, Missouri,
Saloon(s),
Sanders, Rebecca H.,
Saskatchewan, Canada,
Sawmill,
Saylors (family),
Scarlet Fever,
Schoolhouse,
Shanty,
Shea, Marnie M.,
Shea, Michael "Mike" L.,
Shea, Mrs. Patrick,
Shea Road,
Shea, Timothy,
Shade, Athens County, Ohio,
Shannong, Tim,
Sharpsburg (Ohio),
Simpson, Alfred,
Small pox,
Southern Pacific (SP),
Steam train,
Stewart Dam,
Stewart Station,
Stock subscriptions,
Suicide,
Swaim, Helen,

T

Ten year old girl,
Thompson Family,
Thirty-seventh Congress,
Thirty-eighth Congress,
Thomas,
Thompson, John,
Tolliver, George,
Trestles,
Typhoid Fever,

U

Union Pacific (UP),

V

Vermont,
Virginia,
Vinton County (Ohio),
Vinton County—Wescott Public Library,

W

Walters, Engineer,
Waterloo, Athens County, Ohio,
Washington DC,
Washington-Keeton,
Waxing moon,
Waxler, Emma,
Western Maryland Railway (WM),
West State Cemetery,
West Virginia,
Wheelabout Road,
Wheeling, (W.) Va.,
White beard or bearded,
White gown, outfit, or robe,
Windsor, Hartford County, Connecticut,

A HISTORY OF MOONVILLE, OHIO AND A COLLECTION OF ITS HAUNTING TALES

Williams, Bertha,
Williams, Frances M.,
Wolf, Dr.,
Worthington (Ohio) Public Library,

Z

Zaleski (Ohio),
Zaleski, Peter,
Zaleski State Forest,
Zanesville Business College,
Zanesville, Muskingum County, Ohio,

Y

Yardmen,
Yellow lantern,